CW00543298

DEPRESSED ANONYMOUS

Depressed Anonymous

The story of

The Men and Women Who
Have Recovered from Depression

THIRD EDITION

DEPRESSED ANONYMOUS PUBLICATIONS - LOUISVILLE

Depressed Anonymous Publications – Louisville
P. O. Box 17414 Louisville Kentucky 40217
©1998 by Depressed Anonymous
All Rights Reserved
Printed in the United States of America
Published May 1998, July 2008, November 2011

07 06 05 04 03 02 01 00 99 98 IO9 8 7 6 5 4 3 2 1

Parts of this book appeared in a different version in *Depressed? Here is a
Way Out!* 1990 USA © by Earth and Sky Enterprises and in Great Britain
1991 © Fount Paperbacks Foreword © Dorothy Rowe 1991

ISBN 1-929438-14-1

Dedication

This book is dedicated to the many persons who are "carrying the message of hope" to those still suffering from depression.

Contents

The Twelve Steps

Personal Stories

How 31 individuals recovered from the experience of depression.

Appendices

Preface

This work was first published in the United States in 1990 under the title: *Depressed? Here is a way out!*

The second edition appeared under the same title: *Depressed? Here is a way out!* It was published in 1991 by Fount Paperbacks, a division of Harper Collins Publishing Group, Ltd., located in London, England. This edition became out of print in 1995.

Five years from the founding of *Depressed Anonymous* in 1985, the few groups that were operating at that time felt a need for our fellowship to have their own handbook with material directly related to the discussion of depression. This handbook outlined a personal and group recovery plan utilizing the suggested Twelve Step principles of *Alcoholics Anonymous*. We believe that those persons who are looking for a way out of their depression will most surely find our way one that works, if adhered to one day at a time.

Now, with hundreds in the fellowship and more joining weekly, we felt a need to revise the earlier editions by adding more personal stories as well as changing the title to *Depressed Anonymous*. We felt that the new title would give us a more immediate recognition by those who were already involved in a Twelve Step recovery program.

Our program is very simple. There are no fees or dues. All we ask of the newcomer is that they have a desire to leave the prison of their own depression. Likewise, it has been our experience over these past twelve years that those persons depressed and who keep coming back to our fellowship, week after week, always get better. We find that our good days are more frequent and our bad days begin to diminish. That's our promise.

In 1986 there were only two *Depressed Anonymous* groups. Now at this time, there are groups worldwide. It appears that more persons depressed are finding our way helpful.

This book is written by those of us who have been depressed and who have now recovered. We want to share our story about our journey the way it was when we were depressed, and the way it is today. Being part of a circle of hope-filled fellowship is what keeps us centered on our own recovery while at the same time reaching out to others. We believe that to remain un-depressed, we must continue to be open, honest and willing to follow the suggested principles of our Twelve Step program. *Depressed Anonymous* has given us a choice to either choose to stay isolated, or to begin to risk abiding in the warmth of a caring fellowship.

If any of you who are reading about our program of recovery want to learn more about who we are, and what we do, please feel free to write, call or email us. Appendix E will give you the necessary information where you can reach us. We also look forward to hearing from any of you in the medical or mental health fields and/or those of you who have a special interest in the area of spirituality or religion.

Foreword

Dr. Dorothy Rowe, Ph.D., is an international authority on the subject of depression. She writes about her understanding of depression and the part that mutual support groups, such as *Depressed Anonymous* play in the recovery from the prison of depression. This piece by Dr. Rowe served as the Forward to the second edition of *Depressed? Here is a way out!* which was published in 1991 by Fount Paperbacks, a division of Harper Collins Publishing Group, Ltd., located in London, England.

Depression is the greatest misery, for in it we are alone in a prison from which there seems to be no escape. When we have a physical illness, no matter how great our pain, at times we can separate ourselves from our suffering and feel close to other people, sharing a joke, feeling loved and comforted. But when we are in the prison of depression, we cannot separate ourselves from the depression, and there is always a barrier between ourselves and other people.

People who are depressed describe this prison in many different pictures: "I'm at the bottom of a black pit." "I'm locked in a dungeon and they've thrown away the key." "I'm inside a black balloon and as much as I struggle, I can't escape." "I'm alone in an icy desert." "I'm totally alone, and a great black bird is on my shoulders, weighing me down." The pictures are many and various, but the meaning is always the same. The person is alone in a prison.

Even worse, inside the prison of depression, we turn against ourselves in self-hatred. We torture ourselves with guilt, shame, fear and anger. We tell ourselves that we shall never escape from the prison, and indeed, in some way, we do not want to leave the prison. It is torture. It is safety.

The prison of depression is torture because it is isolation, the one form of torture which, as all tortures know, will break even the strongest person. But it is safety because the walls of the prison shut out most of the things which threaten to overwhelm us and cause our very self to shatter and disappear.

Many depressed people will say: "I don't know why I am depressed. It just happened suddenly, like a black cloud coming down." They say this because they do not want to look at the terrible events which threatened to destroy the way they saw themselves and their world. These events might not seem very significant to other people, but to the person concerned, they are very important. It is not the events in themselves which make them important, frightening, or overwhelming, but the meaning we give to these events.

We live in the world of meaning which we have created. Indeed, as individuals, we are our world of meaning. This is why, when we discover a serious discrepancy between what we thought reality was and what it actually is, we feel that our very self is being overwhelmed, is shattering, and disappearing.

With this sense that our self is being annihilated comes the greatest fear, the worst fear we can know. It is greater than the fear of death. We can face death courageously when we feel that some important part of us – our soul or spirit, or our children, or work, or just the certainty that people will remember us – will continue on. But when we feel that it will be as if we never existed, then we feel the utmost terror.

We have to defend ourselves against this terror. In my book: *Beyond Fear*, I have described the many defenses we can use. One of the most popular defenses is depression. Indeed, the human race would not have survived if we did not have the capacity to get depressed. In the safety of the prison of depression, we give ourselves the time and space where we can review the situation and see whether we can arrive at a meaning for ourselves and our life, which will allow us to go on with our lives and to live in some degree of safety and happiness. This is why many people regard their experience of depression as the most important time in their life, for out of that experience, they gained great wisdom.

However, many people are not able to do this because to review their life, they have to remember many painful events and question the actions of those people who should have cared for them. Too frightened to question, they willingly accept the advice of their doctors (who are also frightened to question their own lives) that they have a physical illness, and that the best treatments are pills and electroconvulsive therapy (ECT).

Fortunately, an increasing number of depressed people are realizing that, while making a journey of self-discovery on your own is difficult, making such a journey in the company of other people is a rich, fulfilling experience and leads to enlightenment. These other people might be therapists and counselors, or they may be people who have made, or are making their own way out of the prison of depression.

What we need to look at and question in our lives is how we learned to think of ourselves as being unacceptable, perhaps even bad, and needing to work hard to be good. We certainly did not think that about ourselves when we were born.

At workshops on depression, I ask the people there to remember an incident in childhood which led them to draw the conclusion that they were bad and unacceptable. Only those people who wish to insist that they had a perfectly happy childhood and that their parents were absolutely perfect cannot do this. Such people are few. Most people recall incidents which now might seem funny but then, and now, are sad. All children suffer so much pain and humiliation, even at the hands of parents who love them and want only the best for them.

The way children cope with pain and humiliation and the feeling that they are bad and unacceptable is to promise themselves that if they work hard at being good, when they grow up, they will be rewarded. Indeed, this is what their parents and teachers tell them. They say: "If you are bad, you will be punished, and if you are good, you will be rewarded." Some parents say this in the context of: "This is how the family operates." But most parents and all religions expect children to learn this, not just as a rule to follow at home and at school, but as the principle on which the universe is built. We are taught that the universe is constructed on a Grand Design where goodness is rewarded and badness is punished. Just what the rewards and punishments will be, varies from one religion to another (a good Muslim goes to paradise, a good Hindu is reborn as a wealthy man, a bad Christian goes to hell), but the message of all religions is the same: "If you are good, you will be safe and rewarded. If you are bad, bad things will happen to you."

Such children who absorb this teaching (and most do) become obedient and good. This means that they have to give up much of what they want to do and be, but they comfort themselves that by being good, they will be safe and that their rewards will come.

Children work out all of this in the context of planning what their life will be. We all do this in childhood, some of us very specifically, some of us in very general terms. We create a life project, which is a mixture of what we would like to do and be, what our family wants us to do and be, what options we have, and how we see we can get our just rewards. Most girls create a life project built on the promise: "If you are feminine, unassertive, unselfish and attractive, one day "Mr. Right" will come along, fall in love with you and marry you, and then you'll live happily ever after." Most boys create a project built on the promise: "If you are strong, masculine and competitive, you will win the prize of women, wealth, and power, and other men will admire you."

So, having created our project, we set out to live it.

If we are very very very lucky, the life we live coincides with the project we have created. Very few of us are so lucky. Most of us discover, sooner or later, that there is a discrepancy between what we thought our life would be and what it actually is.

For some of us, the discrepancy is not so great and we can find ways of living with it. Some women discover that their marriage is not happiness ever after, but they console themselves by accepting that their husband, although boring, is a good man and worth putting up with for the sake of the children. Some men discover that not winning all the glittering prizes does not matter if you have mates, a sport to follow, and a comfortable home.

But for many of us the discrepancy is too big, too serious to be smoothed over by consolations, because the cause of the discrepancy is a disaster.

Sometimes the disaster creeps up on us slowly, as gradually the evidence mounts that our expectations of reward are not going to be fulfilled. Perhaps we gradually discover that our marriage is cruel and destructive, or that the job we worked so hard to get is stultifying and meaningless, or that no matter how good we are, our parents will never tell us that they love us unconditionally. Sometimes the disaster comes suddenly with a death, or loss, or when we are betrayed, rejected, abandoned by those most dear to us.

When disaster strikes us, we cry: "I've been good all my life. Why did this happen to me?"

If we believe in the Grand Design of the universe, where goodness is rewarded and badness is punished, there are only two answers we can give: Either the Grand Design was not operating properly, other people are to blame, and we have been treated unjustly; or the Grand Design was operating properly and we are wicked and deserve our punishment.

If we choose the first answer, we feel anger, resentment and bitterness. If we choose the second answer, we feel guilt and shame.

Alternating between these answers, we find all these terrible feelings crowding in on us.

Someone may suggest to us a third answer that the disaster happened by chance. If this is so, does that mean that no amount of goodness prevents disasters? How can I protect myself in a world where disasters can happen by chance? If things can happen by chance, is there no Grand Design? Did my parents and teachers lie to me?

To put an end to this terrifying confusion and the feeling that our very self is shattering and disappearing, we can opt for one answer: "It was my fault and I deserve my punishment," and so, turning on ourselves, cut ourselves off from everybody and everything and find a barren safety in the prison of depression.

To find our way out of the prison of depression we have to recover the sense of acceptability and wrath with which we were born. We cannot do this so long as we cling to the belief in the Grand Design of rewards and punishments, for as much as we tell ourselves that we are acceptable and valuable, we shall continue to take personally all the cruelty and injustices we have suffered. So long as we take these personally, we shall be trapped by anger, bitterness and resentment, just as seeing ourselves as deserving punishment traps us in guilt and shame. To give up taking the cruelty and injustices we have suffered personally, we have to see ourselves, not as a tragic victim of a malign fate, but as simply "unlucky." We were unlucky to have been born into that particular family at that particular time (the family would, however, have treated any baby born to them in the same way as we were treated), unlucky to have met certain people, been in certain places. Nevertheless, having been unlucky in the past does not mean that we shall always be unlucky. In a universe where things happen by chance, we can always be lucky.

To give up our belief in the Grand Design of rewards and punishments, we have to make a journey which many religious people down through the centuries have made. We have to move from the security of the fundamentalist interpretation of the religion to the freedom of the mystical interpretation of the religion.

Every religion has its fundamentalists and its mystics. The fundamentalist interpret their religion in terms of a set of absolute laws which punish the bad and reward the good and which represent the known will of the Supreme Power, God or Allah. The mystics do not have a set of absolute laws (this is why the fundamentalists disapprove of the mystics and often persecute them), and they see the Supreme Power as something or someone who is essentially unknowable but who should be taken on trust. This Supreme Power is not engaged in watching us and keeping a tally of our good and bad deeds, but is simply all around us and within us. All we have to do is let ourselves become aware of this Divine Presence, something we can do with prayerful meditation, and then as Julian of Norwich said: "All shall be well, and all manner of things shall be well."

Many people who are not at all religious have arrived at this same understanding. They experience themselves as being part of everything that is, and while they know that they can never know all that is; they live within the great Oneness with trust and acceptance.

People arrive at this acceptance, trust and understanding in many different ways. Some arrive there through suffering and trying to understand their suffering. Hugh is once such person. Some arrive through the kind of spiritual awareness which Alister Hardy and David Hay have described in their research into religious or spiritual experiences which "give a deep awareness of a benevolent non-physical Power which appears to be partly or wholly beyond and far greater than the individual self." Some arrive there through sudden insight. One of my friends unlocked the door of her depression when she realized that being loved by God, which she had never doubted all through her suffering, was identical with loving yourself.

In his book *The Perennial Philosophy*, Aldous Huxley showed how this knowledge of oneness belonging, no strife or striving, has been described in many different ways, using different kinds of language. We each need to find our own language, and need to acknowledge that what we know can be expressed in many different ways. Hugh uses the language of Christianity, while I find the words of the Tao te Ching come closer to what I feel:

> Express yourself completely
> then keep quiet.
> Be like the forces of nature:
> when it blows, there is only the wind,
> when it rains, there is only the rain,
> when the clouds pass, the sun shines through.
> If you open yourself to Tao,
> you are at one with the Tao,
> and you can embody it completely.
> If you open yourself to insight,
> you are at one with insight,
> and you can use it completely.
> If you open yourself to loss,
> you are one with loss,
> and you can accept it completely.
> Open yourself to Tao,
> then trust your natural responses,
> and everything will fall into place.

Once we have reached such an understanding and acceptance, we want to help other people find this too. I do this chiefly through writing, but Hugh S. does do by action, by engaging people in dialogue, and by getting depressed people to do what they least want to do: to come out of their isolation, to share their experiences with others, and to become concerned with and involved in the lives of other people.

When I first began researching depression, back in 1968, the only treatments that depressed people got from psychiatrists were pills, ECT and psychosurgery, where incisions were made in the frontal lobes of their brain. My research required that I should talk to depressed patients, and lo and behold, many of these patients got better. This was not because I had some magic cure, but because for the first time, these people were able to tell their story to someone who was concerned and interested. By telling their story, they found that their lives gained in significance, and by explaining the whys and hows to someone who was not always sure that she understood, they worked out better choices for themselves, and went on with their lives.

In 1972, I went to Lincolnshire, and there I met a most remarkable young woman, Jackie Childs, who, having been depressed and experienced the horrors of an old fashioned psychiatric hospital, decided that she would try to help depressed people to avoid such suffering by starting a self-help group. I badgered several of my clients into joining, and I followed the progress of the group over several years. I saw many people who spent some time in this group change enormously and take charge of their lives.

At the same time, two organizations, *Depressives Associated* and *Depressives Anonymous*, were established in the UK. *Depressives Associated*, led by the courageous Janet Stevenson who, alas, died in 1990, became a network of people who kept in touch by meetings, letters and telephone, and now a newsletter. *Depressives Anonymous* developed a technique for self-help therapy, and has been a resounding success.

I first met Hugh S. when I was in the USA for a lecture tour in 1986. He invited me to meet the group he had set up in Evansville, Indiana, and we have kept in touch ever since.

There is no need for me to describe what a warm, loving and passionate person Hugh is, because that shines through every page of this book. Nor need I say what a pleasure it is to write a *Forward* to it, because simply knowing that this book is now available to a wide range of readers instead of the lucky few who can join a *Depressed Anonymous* group and work with Hugh is a great pleasure in itself.

Self-help groups for the miseries which plague us can be organized and run successfully in many different ways. Hugh, knowing the *Depressed Anonymous* success of the methods used by *Alcoholics Anonymous*, adapted these to the problems faced by people who are depressed, particularly those who have been depressed for a long time.

This book offers a framework for setting up and running such a self-help group, which can be adapted to the special needs and circumstances of many different people. It can be used as a blueprint for a group or as a study book for an individual. It offers a set of steps and an inexhaustible source of ideas for meditation and discussion. It shows how we can all experience "the miracle of the group." Most of all, it shows how we can discover the essential unity of loving and accepting ourselves and one another, of being close to others, and experiencing the sense of oneness in all in which we can reside in acceptance and trust.

Once we know this, we know that we cannot avoid disaster simply by being good. Since we live on a planet which is not particularly hospitable to us, since we cannot separate ourselves form nor control the political and economic forces of our world, since not all our plans will come to fruition, since events beyond our control may take our loved ones away from us, and old age and death, like taxes, are inevitable, we cannot avoid disaster. But now we are free of the burden of trying to ward off disaster by being good, and we can be good simply because it pleases us to do so. Now we are free of the burden of feeling that we have to pay for every bit of good fortune which befalls us with acts of goodness and a feeling of unworthiness, and we can simply enjoy our good luck. And when disaster strikes, we do not have to ask ourselves what wickedness we have committed. Instead, we meet disaster with courage and with the love and support of our friends.

- Dorothy Rowe

Introduction To Depressed Anonymous

Life is unpredictable! Every living organism operates with a certain amount of unpredictability and uncertainty. The uncertainty of life creates in us a desire for predictability. If we did not believe in the possibility of change, we would all be hopelessly lost and forever bored. Hope would be lost. Potential for a better life would never exist. When there is hope, change is possible. The experience of depression is much the same. Depression is so predictable and unchanging that we lose hope for the pain of our isolation ever coming to an end.

What it was like. More than ten years ago, I began to notice that something was very wrong with the way I was feeling. I can tell you exactly the place and the time when a terrible sadness began to swallow me up. I felt myself, without warning, sliding down and into the dark pit from which I was not able to climb out for a year of painful months. Feelings of inner pain and numbness descended upon me and began to rule my life.

At the time, I thought this descent into hell came from "out of the blue," but like all feelings we experience, I knew that because of situations in my personal past, my emotional reservoir was overdrawn. My reactions to these situations had allowed thoughts and feelings to accumulate a wealth of debt whose note had come due.

I gradually found it more difficult to get out of bed in the morning. I began to experience a feeling of hollowness of spirit gnawing at me from the inside, much like an out of control cancer. This black mood was eating away all that once interested me and I began to feel helpless and out of control. I felt that I was no longer able to retain mastery over my own life.

This painful sadness began to grow gradually from a small unnoticed seed and was unconsciously nurtured to full and frightening heights by my own life choices. It overwhelmed my mind and spirit. My life had become unmanageable. Finally, I had to admit that I was powerless over that something which began to have a life of it's own. Looking back over my life and experiences, I discovered that my thoughts produced the feelings, the feelings produced the moods and the moods produced my behaviors. The mind-body connection is never as much in evidence as it is in this human experience that we label depression.

My depression, with its concomitant restlessness and despair, had been developing gradually over a period of a few months as one loss after another began to accumulate: the loss of a relationship with a woman friend; the fact that my dad was dying; leaving a career of twenty years; having to say goodbye to hundreds of friends; struggling inwardly with having to move back in with my parents at middle age and depending on them for help. At the time I moved back home my dad was recuperating from a massive heart attack and his health was failing fast. This was a great personal loss to me.

Within a month of returning home, I entered a local University and started work on a Master's degree in Counseling Psychology. The studies did not come easy. A few months after I started my degree, I found employment in an entry level position, assisting minority persons who were unemployed. Because of political infighting, this position came to be burdensome. I earned my degree, left my job and moved into private practice. Shortly after that, I began to feel like I was walking into a fog. My mind was blank and my feelings were continually on edge. I felt as if a large hole with jagged edges was located between my gut and my throat. The pain that this produced became a daily reminder that something was not right. The anxiety and jitteriness was enhanced when I began having trouble getting out of bed in the morning. I also had this strong desire to go to bed as soon as I got off work. I could hardly wait to sleep off whatever had me by the throat. I had lost interest in everything and everybody and just wanted to medicate myself with sleep.

The fact that I quit smoking a few months after my dad died was also a large contributing factor in depressing myself. Over the years, the cigarette had become a great friend. This friend was there when I was happy, or when I was nervous, or when I had just finished a meal or had a cup of coffee. It was like an alcoholic who craves just one more drink.

Whatever we humans do must have meaning. I lost my dad; my relationship with my woman friend was over; my role and identity as a Christian minister with a ministry of twenty years. Friends of many years were out of my life, and most important of all, I felt that I had lost myself. I felt alone and worthless. If I saw someone laughing or having a good time, it irritated me. How dare anyone smile while I felt so miserable! The feeling made me think that my brain was made of cotton. I couldn't shove another thought into my head. It was as if the cells of my brain had died.

There was nothing I could do to shake these horrible and painful feelings. My mind was unable to focus on or to concentrate on anything. My memory was affected and it was impossible to retain anything I tried to read. With each new day, I felt my strength ebbing away. I was physically and emotionally drained. I knew that something was wrong – but what was it?

WHAT HAPPENED?

The answer to this question seemed to lie within all the losses that I had accumulated over the past months. I had slipped down into the slippery and dark world known only to someone who has been depressed. I had to do something besides talking to break out of depression. I had to change the way that I lived my life. First, I had to admit that my life was out of control. I was powerless to overcome my symptoms of depression by will power alone. I needed to believe in a power greater than myself. I had to have a spiritual experience. Having been in the ministry for many years, I thought I had a deep spiritual experience, but I seemed to have lost it along the way.

I began to walk five miles a day inside a mall near my home to shake this awful feeling of emptiness that had taken over my very life. I set myself this goal to force myself to walk until I started to feel better. This was about a year following that day in August when I felt myself slipping into the abyss. After doing this exercise of walking day after day for a week, I began to feel a little better. But then the old message came back and said "yes, but this good feeling won't last." Then I knew that since I had good days before the depression, I could have a good day again. I kept on walking, and within time, I walked through the fog that had imprisoned me.

But I had to do the work! Did my symptoms have me imprisoned or did the meaning that I had created in my mind about my life have me imprisoned? I believe it was the meaning that I had given to those losses in my life that gradually threw me to the ground; hog tied me, and wouldn't let me go. I had to believe that somehow my walking gave meaning to the belief that I wasn't going to let these feelings of helplessness beat me down. I just believed that I was going to beat this thing! I learned a great lesson here in that "motivation follows action."

Previous to my own depression, I had worked one on one with a client named Jane. Jane was depressed and confined to her home following quadruple by-pass surgery just weeks before I met with her in her home. I was learning hands-on counseling and my supervisor gave permission for me to practice my counseling skills with Jane. After seeing Jane for ten weeks I saw that she was beginning to improve and began to regain interest in cartooning and poetry writing, things that had given her pleasure before her heart attack. I started thinking if Jane could connect with others who were depressed and participate in a Twelve Step group, she might get better. She might find the same help that other hurting folks who utilize the suggested spiritual principles of a Twelve Step program of recovery have found.

In May of 1985, I started a Twelve Step group known as *Depressed Anonymous.* I had the conviction that a person depressed could find the same strength and serenity as did those who, sick and tired of being sick and tired, had found when they stumbled into their first *Alcoholics Anonymous* meeting. It began as a pilot project at the University where depressed people gathered as a mutual aid group. I discovered that people of all ages, beliefs, and occupations could gradually get out of the prison of depression if they were part of a supportive group, especially if the group followed the suggested Twelve Steps of the group now known as *Depressed Anonymous.* I saw that a Twelve Step program centered specifically around the subject of depression could help people escape isolation and the painful sense of hopelessness. They would no longer feel alone.

WHAT IT'S LIKE TODAY:

All members of the pilot group got better after a number of months of meeting together and applying the Twelve Steps to their lives. Others started to come, and this was the beginning of a group that is now slowly spreading from place to place and from community to community.

Those of us who have lived with depression on a daily basis know despair. For those who have depended principally on drugs and therapy and have found no relief – then this program is a good place for you. For those who have the courage to stay and are willing to go to any lengths to have what we have found, then this personal faith and persistence of yours will begin to pay off. That's a promise from us to you!

Once I finally admitted that I was powerless and began to act out of a belief that I wasn't God, it was quite a relief to surrender my trust to a Higher Power (Steps 1-3)!

Many of us have suffered for so long that we want a quick fix now. It doesn't work that way. You will hear the success stories of those who have returned week after week and "worked" the Twelve Steps to recovery. You can read personal stories of hope and renewal in this book.

We now have a solution to offer those who want to reach out and grasp onto this new way of life, a life that is now focused on recovery and a feeling of hope. With this offer and solution daily before our eyes, we are beginning to see that the depressed have to depend on that spiritual experience in order to really be free from that debilitating scourge of depression. It is this spiritual experience, coupled with the power of the fellowship of those like ourselves where we neither need to explain or excuse ourselves or apologize for being depressed that is the basis for our recovery.

You must want to begin this journey seriously enough to actually take those beginning steps. Someday I hope to know you as a kindred spirit in recovery.

Therapists' Views On Depressed Anonymous

The "Birth" Of A Depressed Anonymous Group.

Judith Bouffiou, PhD. (Cand.), Olympia, Washington

Isn't life just full of expected and unexpected challenges, synchronous happenings, joys and grief? Your life and mine. Following is a synopsis of a time in my life when I experienced all of the above.

The summer of 1991 saw the dissolving of a business partnership for me - a painful, but healthy decision. The counseling center that my ex-partner and I operated had provided the community with a *Domestic Violence/Anger Management (DV/AM) Program* for court and self referred clients, plus each of us had a private practice. My decision to dissolve the partnership was motivated by a number of reasons, among them a desire to go back to school, and to spend more time and energy in my private practice. Over time, my private practice had evolved into a growth and development type of practice, which I loved doing. Along with the dissolution of the partnership came the decision to no longer do the *Domestic Violence/Anger Management* work. I had a desire to still give the community some type of community service, but what?

Then I remembered reading some time earlier in one of my professional journals about a man who had developed a Twelve Step program, *Depressed Anonymous* for individuals who suffered from depression. Like most therapists, a significant number of the people I saw (and still see) in my practice were experiencing depression to one degree or another.

The more I thought about the concept of *Depressed Anonymous*, the more intrigued I was, so I contacted the founder of *Depressed Anonymous* for information and details. Information was sent to me and that was the start of the first *Depressed Anonymous* group in Washington State.

From the *Depressed Anonymous* material I received, I photocopied, organized, prepared and advertised. I decided on a start time and date, sent notices to our local paper, our Crisis Clinic, therapists and physicians in this area, tacked up flyers all over town, and of course, lots of word of mouth advertising. The *Depressed Anonymous* group originally met in a group room at my office, and eventually moved to a local church when I moved into a smaller office space.

As a therapist, I organized, started, sponsored, and "mothered" the *Depressed Anonymous* group for a time, before withdrawing to just being the phone contact person that people can call in for information. From the very first meetings, which had 8-10 people, a "home" group evolved; fine people, some of whom had previous Twelve Step experiences. One of the fine traditions and legacies of Twelve Step groups is the willingness of folks to be and do the supportive and necessary work (the glue) that holds the Twelve Step groups together. The Twelve Step tradition and service continues on.

As is often the case, I have received more than I've given as the person who organized and started this Olympia, Washington *Depressed Anonymous* group. Now I'm not a person who suffers from depression, other than short term appropriate situational depression; nothing ever deep or prolonged. As I organized and started this *Depressed Anonymous* group, little did I know that I would benefit from the *Depressed Anonymous* process and group in such a personal way.

The *Depressed Anonymous* group had only met two or three times when my middle son unexpectedly died from a type of cancer which years before had taken his father. So, in a synchronous manner, for a time and in a different way, the *Depressed Anonymous* group supported me as much as I supported them. In my prior work as a nurse, I had often been witness to dying and death, also in my personal life. However, the death of one son and then a year and a half later, the death of my oldest son (two out of three) have been devastating experiences for me.

So in many many ways, being the organizer and sponsor of the first *Depressed Anonymous* group has been an exceedingly enriching experience for me. As mentioned before, because of the wonderful people in the group, and with great confidence on my part, I turned the operation of the *Depressed Anonymous* group over to the capable hands of the home group people. I remain the telephone contact. The *Depressed Anonymous* group continues to thrive and grow. Just recently, I talked with a man from Portland, Oregon, who is thinking about starting a group in the Portland area. I urged him to do so, as I'm sure he'll find his experience as richly rewarding as mine has been.

Thank you for offering me the opportunity to share this positive experience with you.

My Views on Depressed Anonymous

Denise List, M.Ed., Louisville, Kentucky

One of the greatest resources I've used in working with many depressed persons has been *Depressed Anonymous*. The transformation it causes in an individual's life is truly miraculous. This stems from it being primarily a spiritual program of healing and recovery. It encourages a person to seek a personal relationship with God, whoever they understand Him to be. In doing this, it helps a person to look inside for healing, rather than in a pill or some quick "cure." Many persons who suffer with depression look on God as being one who judges them harshly. This thinking usually leads to much anger towards God, which results in more negative thinking. I know this from my own experiences with depression, and the angry relationship with God I had during those times. This is where *Depressed Anonymous* offers hope by getting a person connected to a group who also suffer with depression, and are working the Twelve Steps. In doing this, it helps a person come to a realization that it will only be through a Power greater than themselves that they will find sanity in their life. Depressed people cannot do this alone because of the compulsion to ruminate endlessly over negative thoughts. It is only through coming together with a group of people like *Depressed Anonymous* that they are able to break the cycle of negative thinking.

A client I was working with is a good example of the above. He spent his time alone and many countless hours thinking of all the disappointments in his life, which continually reinforced his depression. Then he started going to *Depressed Anonymous*, and found that through being with other people like himself, he didn't feel as alone as he did before. He started sharing his pain, and found understanding and support. Then I noticed his face began to soften, and he started smiling more. He also found help spiritually from *Depressed Anonymous* , for he started working the Twelve Steps, and as a result, he started trusting God more for his healing.

He is one of many persons I've worked with who have found help and encouragement through attending *Depressed Anonymous*.

The spiritual emphasis of *Depressed Anonymous* is its greatest strength. People come together and hear from one another how their higher power is healing and guiding their lives. They realize that in being part of the group, they are not alone, and also encourage true healing. *Depressed Anonymous* has been a wonderful healing tool in the lives of many depressed persons I've worked with. It will always be one of the greatest resources I use in my work. It is true that "it works if you work it."

Step One

We admitted that we were powerless over depression and that our lives had become un-manageable.

How often have I had people tell me that they've "suffered" from depression for as long as they could remember. They tell of many agonizing hours, days, months and years in which they consider their depression experience as an everlasting problem. Some say that their depression is a comfort, namely that they would be lost without that old and predictable miserable feeling they wake up to every morning. In other words, they have bought into one of the six principles of defeat experienced and lived out by persons depressing – that is to say: "that since bad things have happened to me in the past, bad things will happen to me in the future." They believe that what is will always be.

It is in the admission that we are out of control that a remedy can be applied to our battle with depression. It is a paradox for our understanding of depression to learn that only when we give up control, do we gain control over what we want to be, think and do. If there is anything that creates a sense of hopelessness, it's when we feel that we don't have any control over our lives. When we are depressed, we feel dependent on all the forces that act on us and our environment. We feel that we are the victims of the interminable feeling that we call depression. Depression can be like a hell or bottomless pit from which we feel we can never escape. It's like being in an eighty-foot hole with an eight foot ladder.

Some of the major ways people help build the walls of their depression are to consider themselves worthless, they won't allow themselves to get angry, they can't forgive themselves or others, and they believe that life is bad and death is worse. Also, they believe that since bad things happened to them in the past, bad things are bound to happen to them again in the future.

This is the type of thinking that we must surrender if we want to feel better. We can start enjoying a life that is meant to be enjoyed – not just endured. We especially want folks like yourself to get involved in a group that we call *Depressed Anonymous*. It is one of the better ways to realize that we can choose to escape the terrible personal isolation and anguish of depression. Who better knows the pain and the isolation of depression than the person who has been depressed? It is my personal conviction, both as a psychotherapist and as a person who has experienced depression that it was only when I admitted that I was depressed that I could start working my way out of this terrible and immobilizing experience. In my own experience, I thought I was losing my mind, as I couldn't cram another thought into my head and couldn't remember a thing that I had just read or thought a minute before. I was tired all the time and would wake up early in the morning and couldn't get back to sleep. But that's the best news most people hear when they come to a *Depressed Anonymous* meeting for the first time, namely that they are not losing their minds. When you're depressed, you feel your mind is made out of cottonwool and all of life seems grey, cold and lifeless.

The important thing to remember about depression is that you are not a victim. You have bought into the belief that you can't change how you feel. You need to believe that once you change the way you think then that in itself can begin to produce a change in the way you feel.

Thoughts produce feelings which produce our behavior. Give up the belief that you are like the helpless sailor alone in his boat on the ocean without a paddle. You are not a sailor without a paddle – you do have a paddle, but you feel that since there is no land in sight, it won't make any difference for you to row anyway. So many times people who depress themselves feel that no matter what they do, they will never feel better. With the Twelve Step program, you can recover – although most likely not right away. Let's be honest – nothing that has taken the greater part of a lifetime to build can be dismantled in a few days or weeks. But you will feel better if you follow the instructions in this book and begin to work and live the Twelve Step program.

Persons who come to *Depressed Anonymous* meetings soon learn that if they want to make progress and start to feel good about themselves, then they have to admit that they are powerless over their depression and that their lives have become unmanageable. I might have had the thought – possibly even as I read this – that I want to end my life. Please finish reading this book before you do anything else. Others have been helped and now so can you be. You can make that decision and choose to begin to feel better. You can get out of your depression if you want to – like most depressive experiences, many are due to the way we have learned to think and act. There is no proof – again, let me repeat – there is no scientific proof that shows that a specific and significant change in the brain chemistry proceeds and is the cause of depression. Dorothy Rowe points out that any emotion, pleasant or unpleasant, felt long enough, can produce significant physiological changes in the human body. The implication here is that if you think enough unpleasant thoughts long enough, then these thoughts are bound to have some form of repercussion in the body. We are not talking here about some prescribed medications that have been known to cause the patient to feel depressed.

Dorothy Rowe maintains that if you work out of the *disease model* for your understanding of depression, then the good implication is that you might catch it again, like the flu or winter cold. But Dorothy Rowe sees another model, namely the *psychological model* which helps us better understand the source of human depression. She says that if you operate out of the psychological model instead of the disease model, then the bad implication is that you caused the depression yourself; but the good implication is that if you caused it yourself, then you can un-depress yourself. This is our position in *Depressed Anonymous*.

Depressed Anonymous is based on the Twelve Steps of *Alcoholics Anonymous.* We grant that we are not alcoholics, but we also know that our compulsive depressing thoughts and actions continually reinforce our sense of worthlessness and hopelessness.

Whenever we feel like withdrawing from an unpleasant situation or thought, we immediately medicate ourselves with an immobilizing feeling of sadness. By "medicate," I mean that we use sadness like an anesthetic drug in that it prevents us from feeling anything other than the sadness that is ever present. Any situation that might cause us to live and think differently is sometimes cause enough for us to medicate ourselves with sadness. Many times, just a thought about a past sin or fault of ours will throw us down into a spiral of self-hate and despair. We sadden ourselves. Even though the Twelve Steps of *Alcoholics Anonymous* deal with a person's compulsion to drink, and those in *Alcoholics Anonymous* unequivocally promote the idea that alcoholism is an illness, no one should feel guilty or ashamed of their addiction to alcohol because it is a disease. We in *Depressed Anonymous* do not espouse the idea that persons depressed are mentally ill. This stigma has been placed on persons depressed long enough, and it has stopped many from getting help because of the shame associated with this painful feeling.

In *Depressed Anonymous*, we meet many people who come to our group expecting to hear us say that their depression is an illness or that they are sick. They will not hear that at a *Depressed Anonymous* meeting. We do know that an unpleasant emotion experienced over time, such as fear, can produce metabolic changes in the human body. *Depressed Anonymous* has at its core the Twelve Steps and we advocate their use as the surest way out of depression. The Twelve Steps originated to deal with the baffling and cunning problem of alcoholism. We also see their power work for people who don't have a disease but want to get in touch with a Power greater than themselves so as to recover from their crippling depression. When we tell them that just as they caused their depression they likewise can un-depress themselves, we caution them that this is not intended to put them down but to give them hope. We believe that in time, and by working the program, they will begin to feel better.

Many newcomers only know that their sadness has been a part of their life for as long as they can remember. We do not blame them for their depression. We in *Depressed Anonymous* are not in the blame game. We only want to look our depression squarely in the eye and learn how to get un-depressed. Our recovery from depression depends on our desire to quit saddening ourselves, coupled with the admission that our lives are unmanageable and that only a Power greater than ourselves can free us from our life-long prison of depression.

But don't get me wrong – I don't believe you can snap out of your depression, or suddenly and dramatically get your life turned around by going to one *Depressed Anonymous* meeting, or reading the Twelve Steps five times an hour. It just doesn't happen that way, especially if you have lived with your depression for any length of time. Even though we emphasize that your depression is not a disease, we do want you to know that a depression over a long time can cause physical problems and upset the metabolism of the human organism. More and more, doctors are seeing how positive feelings, attitudes and emotions can help cancer patients maintain a remission and stay free of a recurring cancer condition. Unpleasant emotions such as fear, anger, resentment, tension and depression work against recovery.

I would call this sadness that has been with us for as long as we can remember a learned way to respond to certain negative stimuli. What you will be doing when you come to Depressed Anonymous meetings is to get involved in your own healing. You will find other men and women who are struggling with the same pain as you are. You will discover that the first step in coming to grips with a depression that won't quit is for you to surrender it, quit fighting it. Let the God, as you understand it, take over your life and help let it restore you to sanity, peace and understanding of the way in which you can find the path out of your prison of depression. *Depressed Anonymous* works if you begin the work of the spiritual program that we are going to outline in this book. Depression is a moral problem and as such there needs to be a moral solution, one part of which is to admit that we are responsible for ourselves and that we can't blame it on genes, psychological predispositions or one's spouse. We are going to take charge. We choose to un-depress ourselves. Today! One day at a time!

In the past, we have found that the program works if you keep at it. The best way to keep at it is to attend meetings as often as you can, so that you are able to hear how others have gotten out of their depression and are learning how to stay in touch with their Higher Power. You know there is simply something positive being part of a self-help group and being able to talk about what you are feeling. You do have a choice though, and as Abraham Lincoln was supposed to have said: "You are about as happy as you make up your mind to be." I agree with that. But let me warn you – it isn't easy to do something different from what you have been doing most of your life. That is especially true when it comes to the way we see ourselves, the world and others. There are no magic pills and no easy answers to brings us immediately out of this inner pain and anguish. It does take time and work.

If you really want to leave behind your painful sadness, the daily tears, and the feelings of worthlessness, then begin now to admit the un-manageabless of your depression. You have had it with feeling out of control!

That's the way it is with depression – over the years you get comfortable with feeling miserable, which doesn't mean you like it, but that you're just too afraid to risk feeling something different. When you want to change and leave your depression behind the choice that you want to make is immediately dashed to the ground because you just feel that there is no hope for you. "I can't pull myself up by my bootstraps and start to feel better," you tell yourself. Most of the time, we tell ourselves that we'll do it when we feel better. Folks, let me tell you something – you'll never feel better until you begin to physically get moving! We all know that we feel better only when we get into gear and get busy – distracting ourselves from those ever present miserable thoughts whispering how bad we are and how hopeless life seems to be.

You have to admit that you're powerless over this depressed behavior and likewise admit that your life is unmanageable. You don't want to go on living this way. In fact, some days you feel that you just want to lie down and die, but deep inside you there is that Spirit, call it God, Higher Power, or whatever, that keeps you searching for a way out. A part of you is still hanging on and giving you hope to try to live through this pain of hopelessness and isolation. You just know there has got to be something out there that will give you at least a glimmer of hope. This part of you has been competing for years with those other parts of you that say "End it all," "Give up – you'll never feel better," or worse "You are losing your mind and you can't go through all this for another day."

But listen to that small voice folks – this is the voice that has been trying to be heard for years, only other negative voices and our own old negative mental tapes have had more training in getting their message across. Now that small vice, that little part of you that wants to have light and some hope is getting up the courage to ask more for itself. It tries to get stronger as it attempts to outshine those other parts of ourselves; those parts that have been telling us how trapped we are in our feelings of worthlessness. How often do people say that part of them wants to do this and yet another part of them wants to do that. I believe that is the best expression of the conflict that goes on in many of us when we are depressed. Usually the part that is hurting and sad speaks the loudest and so often gets the most attention – but why not? It's hurting. When that part of us gets hurt, it wants to withdraw – to hide and cry. It's like a small child who wants to run away from all the anguish and disappointment. But inside of us when the parts are struggling with each other, it's like two teams pulling in a tug of war, and that takes energy to keep alive. We get worn out as we continually ruminate about how sad we are feeling and how hopeless everything looks. Most days we just want to go to our room, lie down and sleep. Have you noticed that the more depressed you become, the more sleep you need or don't need? There is that constant jittery feeling that won't go away and whichever reminds us of the hollowness of our lives. The life we live is as bitter as ashes in our mouths.

Let's listen now to the long-denied part of us that speaks out in favor of a change – that voice of hope that says we will feel cheerful one day. The small part of us that says that we should risk going to this meeting and admit that: "Yes, I am depressed, and yes, I am going to find my way out of this prison by taking stock of my strengths and by beginning to want to hope." You do have a choice. You can begin to let go of your fears of what life will be like without this constant gnawing feeling inside of you that produces that awful jitteriness. You will find lots of acceptance from the group as you listen to the many ways others like yourself have surrendered their problems to their Higher Power and have begun to find a peace and sanity that they never thought existed. The old tapes in your head will whisper that there is no hope for you that no one is as badly off as you are, and that nobody will want to help you as you don't deserve anything anyway. Often these old tapes have been with us since childhood and many of our adult depressions have their roots in our childhood. Many people do not remember much of their childhood, but repressing memories does not mean that the emotions belonging to these experiences in childhood disappear.

Depression is sometimes a sign of a lost and un-grieved childhood. Many times our depression stems from a shame, a feeling sad about something that happened to us a long time ago and which has been blocked from our memories because it was at the time too painful to look at. We felt ashamed. We even might have felt that we were a mistake, that we have no right to exist. It still makes us sad.

We can only live now, and so we have to let go of past hurts and past resentments. We can learn that it's OK to tell others what we feel, that we feel bad, that we have given up all hope and that we have tried to do away with our own lives. The group, you will discover, accepts your statements of despair, as they have experienced the very same feelings. You will find acceptance, encouragement and new skills as you begin to form new friendships and slowly begin to believe that maybe you too can feel better with a little time and work. You begin to live with more hope as you hear each member express their feelings of how their life was before *Depressed Anonymous* and how it is now as they practice the Twelve Step program in their daily lives.

Depressed Anonymous means hope – as long as you want to get out of the pit of depression just start to believe that little voice which says: "Yes, I am hopeful, I will feel better too. The other members of Depressed Anonymous give me hope. Others have made it out of the deep lonely pit of depression, and so can I. I choose to be happy even if I don't feel happy right away. I am going to risk feeling different from this wretched sadness that I feel all the time. I have nothing to lose – except my fear of the future."

But with OUR new way of living and thinking we are going to stay in the *now*. We know tomorrow produces anxiety and fear. Yesterday is there with all the old past hurts and anger. All I have is the *now*! If I live in the *now*, I can begin to try to stay out of yesterday with all its old wounds and hurts, and resist living in tomorrow with it's unknown problems. Negative thoughts about our past or those about tomorrow can numb our feelings so that we don't have to feel the pain of whatever it is that isolates us from the world around us. We also admit, like any one person addicted to a person, place, thing, chemical or drug, that our lives are out of control. We have to admit that by depressing ourselves, we have chosen saddening ourselves as our drug of choice. We medicate ourselves with sadness any time we might have to change the way we live our lives. Sometimes, our depression or sadness arises out of guilt as we continue to turn our personal mistakes into giant catastrophes – this continues to make us feel as if we're nothing and valueless. This all adds to our frustration and the feeling of our being out of control. We know that if we just give up our struggle against depression and admit our powerlessness over it, we can begin to surrender it to our Higher Power and practice letting go of it. I can decide that I want to feel good again. I can decide that I want to feel happy and put this constant sadness and hollowness behind me once and for all. I know that no longer will I have to retreat or flee from these sad feelings and escape with sleep, over-activity or drugs. I know that, whenever my sadness seems unending, I then just admit that I am not helpless and that I can do something about it because I have the tools and I can learn the skills that I didn't know were available to me before. Now I am deciding to think, act and behave differently, much to my personal credit and a new-found trust in the Higher Power. I am a sailor who sees the land, knows the right direction and does the rowing to get where I want to get. The Twelve Steps are my compass. I also know that this group of people which we call *Depressed Anonymous* will help me assume a sense of no longer feeling out of control.

Instead, I believe that I will begin to take responsibility for my life and risk getting better. In time, I can trust the group with my story and my struggles against the heaviness of daily life. In time, I can trust God to take away my hurts and pains and sadness, just as I have begun to trust the members of *Depressed Anonymous* with my deepest hurts and feelings of loneliness.

This first step is really the most important step in that we admit that our lives are out of control – that our lives are un-manageable – that we need to believe that we now have to make a choice for our own happiness. We can continue to dwell in the mire, the self-pity of depression, or we can begin to work with others and see that there is hope for our depression.

The starting point is the admission that so far everything we have tried has not worked. How often have I heard members of *Depressed Anonymous* say that since coming to *Depressed Anonymous* their lives have become less sad and they feel more hopeful. Some of them have reduced their antidepressant medication, and have had their doctors get them off the medication altogether. I believe the proof is in watching the person in the program who, week after week, gradually begins to show improvement. All improvement comes slowly – thank God for that or we couldn't handle it! I have noticed that people who continually work their program and surrender to a Higher Power begin to look different – that's right – they look different. They begin to seem more relaxed and their faces begin to assume a softness – a new radiance. I can tell that they are getting better, and the group lets them know how much better they look. It's good to get positive feedback that we are doing something right.

The God that we know speaks to us through members of the *Depressed Anonymous* group. The Higher Power will put a new sense of purpose into your life once you know how to turn to it and surrender your pain. The *Depressed Anonymous* will lead you safely and gently! The miracle is in the group.

One of the things that we try to keep from happening in the group is to have people label themselves as "depressives," as if that's what their total being is all about. No, we are more than just people who are experiencing depression – we are also people who are working on this sadness in ourselves and we continue to surrender it to the Higher Power or God as we understand God. To say that we are "a depressive" is like a woman who says that she is just "a housewife," as if this particular role makes her all that she is. Also, sometimes the recovering alcoholic says he or she is just an alcoholic; no, they are more than an alcoholic. We never want to have a single kind of behavior limit who we are – or define our identity. We are more than any one behavior, even though that one might influence the rest of our behavior. Once we admit that our depressed thinking is what conditions us to see our world as a hopeless place to live, the more we will try to change the way we think. What we want to accomplish in *Depressed Anonymous* is to listen to those folds who are working their program who experience a new sense of control over their feelings and appreciate and learn new skills that help them from going into the depths of depression once again.

Some people say that once a person gets un-depressed that should help them to no longer need the meetings and fellowship of the group – but that's like telling the alcoholic that he/she can drink again after so many weeks of *Alcoholics Anonymous* and working the Twelve Steps. This is where the addictions have so much in common with each other. Addictions also have the same characteristic in that they are used so as to allow an individual to escape a painful reality or stressful experience. Another addiction is smoking, and it us used to help people cope with stressful situation. I also see overeating as an addiction because it helps people stuff the pain and emptiness which they find in their lives. In like manner, depression can be used as an escape from the reality of living a life filled with uncertainty and risk. No wonder depression is such a hellish experience because it is always the same, and the people who are severely depressed have convinced themselves with their circular way of thinking that life will never get better and that they are doomed to this sadness with its continual hurt and pain. You only can hope where there is uncertainty and unpredictability in one's life. With depression, one is faced with a hell of isolated sadness. But this is where the first step comes into play for all of us who have been depressed and who are struggling to free ourselves from its grip. We are hooked on an addictive behavior and a habitual way of thinking when we continue to depress ourselves – we have opted for the belief that this fleeing sadness is the only way to live our lives. Could we say that we are saddicts? Withdrawal into addictive behavior and thinking is what keeps us from facing the reality of living a life filled with hope and peace.

Like with any addictive behavior, we have to continue to focus on ourselves and the ways to stay spiritually connected with God's will for us as we go about our daily lives. There must be a continued practicing of the Twelve Steps, as they are the force that keeps us ever alert from falling back into all the old ways of thinking and acting, which cause us to remain sad and keep us from having to make the choice of being happy. Just as the people who are addicted to gambling, eating, alcohol or depression follow the Twelve Steps and take to heart the need for a continual turning of their lives over to the Higher Power for wisdom, guidance and serenity, so does the person who is an active member of *Depressed Anonymous*. The *Depressed Anonymous* member has no reason to fear talking out with members of the group his or her need to use sad and defeating thinking to punish themselves for being so worthless and bad.

One of the more constant behaviors of the individual depressing is to engage in fewer and fewer pleasant activities. The person depressed just can't bring himself or herself to do anything that might cause a sense of elation or pleasure. If you feel that you are bad, worthless and without any value, then you can't get yourself to do something that might make you have a good feeling about yourself. An individual depressing can make himself or herself feel anxious, sick and even faint. With the support of a group like *Depressed Anonymous*, one can begin to see that life doesn't have to be lived alone in agony or misery, and that is precisely the miracle of the group. You begin to see that you can stay parked in neutral in your misery and feel hopeless or you can step out in faith as most members of the group do, and admit that you've had it with this sadness and begin to choose life. I do believe a renewed sense of hope is in our hands – we can choose to be sad or we can choose to live with purposeful joy. It's a risk we choose to take.

I remember a client who once told me that he was afraid to come to DA because he imagined everyone there was probably filled with self-pity and had sad tales to tell. "Why depress myself more?" he asked. I suggested that Ralph go and try a couple of meetings before he gave his negative verdict on the group. He went to a meeting, expressed his feelings of surprise that they had said aloud what he felt, and went back time and time again. He said that it was the first time he could go to a place where everyone accepted him for what he was, and they didn't say that he was crazy or losing his mind as he shared his experience of depression. He knew as well as I did that depression can cause one to lose the ability to concentrate as well as to remember things. It's a secure feeling to hear that someone else has had the same experience as your own. Going to a *Depressed Anonymous* meeting when you're depressing is like going to a foreign county and finding someone who speaks your language. When you speak depression the group knows the language.

This is the first step – to surrender and admit that your depression has made your life unmanageable and miserable. Acknowledge that your life is indeed unmanageable and proceed onto the next step, where you know that you don't have it in your will power to turn it around but that only the Higher Power or God, as you understand God, can remove your sadness and despair. You have the choice! Make a decision to want to feel better – today!

Step Two

Came to believe that a Power greater than ourselves could restore us to sanity.

What do we consider to be the Higher Power or the God that is larger and more powerful than our personal depression? In our prayer we believe that God or the Higher Power can free us from the burden of our joylessness, and that the why of our depression is not as important as the fact that we are depressed. What is it about our complete dependence on this obsession with sadness, our chronic fatigue and feelings of worthlessness that won't let go of us? Granted, sometimes we feel depression is a comfort, and we're afraid to let go of it because we don't as yet know what will replace it. Hope tends to be unpredictable whereas the pain of depression is constant and predictable. We can depend on it.

We have given ourselves over to the belief that this growing feeling of helplessness is what must govern our lives, moods and behavior. We have given it license to run roughshod over every part of our life and over our relationships. Most people can't see inside us and discover the pain that makes up our every waking moment. For the most part we are able to hide how miserable we feel.

Our awareness is constantly shifting inside ourselves to monitor our every mood as it shifts from anxiety to fear, from anger to rage and back to sadness – our sadness and helplessness make us feel angry about how boxed in we always feel. All parts of us in pain cry out for attention.

We learn that there is a God who is supposed to love us and take care of us, but we are afraid to let go of who we believe we are or what we feel we have to be. Trust is something that we have given up a long time ago. Trust is hard for us, especially when we feel that life, people and our circumstances have completely let us down. For so long now, unpleasant feelings have led us to believe that we have no right to happiness, now or in the future. We have grown up with a sense of suspicion of those around us who appear happy and satisfied with life. Instead we find it safer to back away from too much involvement with other people, because they would see how bad we really are if they got to know us and then our secret would be out. We don't ever know what "normal" feels like because we constantly feel so hollow and empty inside.

We now know that once we have taken that first step and admitted we are powerless because of our depression and simply believe that our God, as we understand God to be, will restore us to serenity.

Our addiction to turning inside ourselves and feeling sad is just one other way to deny our true situation. In reality, we have become saddicts! Whenever we want to be comforted we turn to this feeling of powerlessness which continues to validate our sense of worthlessness.

If we want to continue feeling that we are not good, bad and worthless, this type of negative thinking can do nothing but produce the self-fulfilling prophecy, namely, that we will never feel good. When we begin to to look at our strengths, listen to other people who were once depressed, we can begin to see a glimmer of light and hope coming along our path. We also can begin to believe this force, Higher Power, God is asking us to give hope a chance in our despairing lives. We begin to hear the older members of the *Depressed Anonymous* group share how they began to put their trust in something bigger than themselves and were ready to move out of the pain of their small, painful worlds and begin to grow. This power that is greater than our self could be members of the *Depressed Anonymous* group, a book, Jesus, or whatever a person wants to make it. Most persons working the Twelve Steps for whatever addiction or co-dependency admit that it is their dependence on the Higher Power that keeps them sober, serene and balanced. As their trust level goes up so does their mood.

It's and addiction if you find yourself continually bashing yourself for past mistakes and/or failures. It is this constant rumination that puts us in the negative spiral which leads to more isolation, withdrawal and psychic pain. The familiar feeling of sadness and the continual inner hollowness that make our life so miserable becomes our security.

Often when we are closely intertwined with some compulsive/addictive behavior, it isn't until we let go of the pain that drives our depression that original pain, hurt, guilt or shame gradually melts away. In the group meeting each of us begins our new directions by listening to older Twelve Step people who speak openly and honestly about the time when they were so depressed that they couldn't even get out of bed and sleep away their unending misery. Some people have a difficult time trusting those people who work their program and who say that they would feel better if they continue, attend meetings, work their Twelve Step program, eat properly, get an exercise program and talk about their sadness with others. They keep themselves imprisoned in their depression by continually repeating to themselves that since nothing has worked in the past why should something good happen now?

At each *Depressed Anonymous* meeting we hear different members of the group tell how their Higher Power helped return them to a peace, a serenity that they had never experienced until they started coming to *Depressed Anonymous* and began working on themselves. Now they can spend time in prayer and meditation with the Higher Power guiding their lives through the times of darkness. In time they have found giving up their depression to the care of the Higher Power almost a pleasure. It is our belief that if we want to begin to live, we must surrender our addiction to depression. The more we are tempted to seek comfort and bash ourselves with thoughts of how bad we are, the more depressed we become. But on the positive side the more we begin to take mastery over our thinking and our listless behavior, the smaller, gradual gains we will make in seeing some light at the end of the tunnel by living just for today, that is, one day at a time, and not in the hurts and anger of yesterday or the fear and anxiety of tomorrow, we will begin to see a spark of light coming over the horizon.

Looking around at the group and listening to the stories of how they are feeling better and doing better by just keeping their lives simple and less cluttered. The persons who begin to leave the prison of depression are the ones who desire a change and are taking the appropriate steps to gain their freedom. Ever since they came into the group they have heard how one person after another had been helped by their belief that a Power greater than themselves can restore them to some sort of serenity and peace.

Dorothy Rowe says that some depressed people wish to be a martyr and give a thousand and one reasons why they should stay depressed. They can think up thousands of painful thoughts about how bad they are and how they don't deserve the cheer and joy that most of us frequently experience in our daily lives. Some run over and over again in their minds the awful things that they have done, and become used to their continual ruminating over their own sense of worthlessness. They have fallen into the depressed person's morbid need to feel bad. The sadness continues to eat away at the very heart of the person until there is no more hope and the light at the end of the tunnel has been snuffed out. In their hopelessness of ever getting better, they throw away the only key that will unlock their prison, and that is the key called hope. Getting to the hope is at the heart of getting our lives and feelings reorganized. We begin to believe that maybe I too can overcome my depression like other members of the group. Not only am I consciously changing the way I think but likewise I am forcing myself to get involved with the other members of the group and am making friends. I know that withdrawing from others is one of the first signs that we are depressing ourselves. But it is in the continual contact with others like myself that I can begin to find a way out of my depression.

If all I can believe in is my own sense if feeling inadequate or worthless, then it is time to look for something positive to believe in. we come to believe that there is another way out of this hell which we experience as sadness and emptiness. Once we make a commitment to change the way we think, believe, feel and interact with others, the more we will want to ask the Higher Power for help along our way of recovery. So often in the past we have been so self-reliant that God or the Higher Power didn't have room to move in our lives. We are ever mindful that this change takes time but in reality we can only live one day at a time. We have to believe that this Power will gradually allow us to feel and act differently, and by that I mean it will allow us to act with hope. The more that we trust ourselves to feel hopeful, the greater the possibility that our depression will pass. We know that our feeling sad is related to our thinking sad thoughts, and many times we aren't even conscious why we are feeling sad and down.

The group helps us share with each other our feelings of isolation, and *Depressed Anonymous* is a group which addresses itself solely to depression and the group's success as a group comes honestly. We say who we are and make no apologies. We know that when we share with others our story of depression they know what we are talking about because they have been there. The group doesn't sugarcoat the task of turning our depressive lifestyle around. Most people, including our family and close friends, want to tell us to snap out of our depression, as though we can just turn the feelings of sadness and hopelessness on and off like a tap. The key again is to admit first of all that we are depressed and then believe that the Higher Power can restore us to sanity.

The sanity of the Twelve Step program is what will eventually help you change how you look at yourself and your experience of depression. The program shows that just because you have always felt miserable is no reason to remain miserable for the rest of your life. The sanity of placing your trust in a Power greater than yourself opens up great possibilities for your personal happiness and success. If you have felt you had to be in total control of every situation in your life, then coming to believe in a Power greater than yourself might be a frightening experience. What would happen if suddenly you couldn't control your unhappy situation with the comfort of sadness or self-pity? Haven't our sadness and thoughts of unworthiness been our last refuge from having to face ourselves, take charge and accept responsibility for our own lives?

The escape into feelings of worthlessness and resignation over my depressing feelings is no longer an acceptable way for me to delay the hard choice of being responsible for me. This statement is not made to make you feel guilty but only to help you see that, with time and by working the Twelve Steps on a daily basis and having the ongoing fellowship and support of the *Depressed Anonymous* group, you can begin to choose a way out.

We have a new way of looking at ourselves in *Depressed Anonymous*. We believe that if I am to feel better and get through this painful experience I call depression, then I'm going to have to surrender some parts of myself that have become like old friends – old friends of the negative and toxic sort. These parts tell me that I am bad, worthless and unable to be happy. You have made these irrational and negative voices the force to live by. Now *Depressed Anonymous* asks you in the second step to begin to make a mental assent to the fact that only a Power greater than yourself can free you from the prison of depression. This power will help you let go of your self-doubts, irrational beliefs and negative self-image. Granted, we want to tell you that change is never easy but only possible when you choose to place your trust in the Higher Power. The miracle of the group is that it will show you that you are important, that you will be accepted, and that you will learn how others in the group with the same experience of depression as your own are now experiencing hope.

This new belief in the Higher Power is not the creation of any organized religion but instead is the Power that creates the universe. Our surrender and trust in it frees it to work its way in our lives. That is the paradox of the Twelve Steps – the more we depend on the Higher Power instead of our addictions, the freer we in reality become.

This new belief will in time give us the power to think about risking life without having to be dead sure of what the next moment will bring. It appears that when we are depressed, we are so sure that since everything in the past has been bad so should everything be in the future. You just expect everything to turn out badly. So, the tomorrows never look very good to us. We need therefore to live in the *now* and it is when we surrender to the Higher Power that we finally begin to feel a safety we never felt before.

We also know that our withdrawal from others has given excessive power to those already entrenched feelings of worthlessness and sadness. It seems that our inactivity and social isolation just help build higher and stronger walls to our prison. This is why we need to hear stories like Bob's, who was one of the original members of *Depressed Anonymous* – he felt that *Depressed Anonymous* was one of the few places where he could laugh, where he could be himself. He was with people who understood him and they didn't consider him crazy or reinforce his own feelings that he might be losing his mind.

Jane was given an ultimatum to get help by her daughter, who saw the *Depressed Anonymous* group as a last chance for her mother, who was suicidal and despondent over the death of her husband a few months earlier. Jane didn't want to come to the meeting - she came only to please her daughter.

She watched everyone at her first meeting and when she saw that they weren't too wired she finally thought she'd throw her story at them toward the end of the meeting. To her surprise no one fell out of their seats. She felt sure that the shock of saying that she'd tried to kill herself twice without success would surely get a rise out of the group. Instead it got people to share their own hard times, and they also shared how the group has continued to help then through hard times. They suggested that Jane keep coming back to the group, and encouraged her with the belief that she would continue to feel better following each meeting.

Jane did keep coming back to the meetings, and she started to look different as her face began to soften and she had a twinkle in her eye as she came to the meetings wanting to give instead of just receive. Now with the support of the group she began to take charge of her life and is an active member, continually telling others how it was and how it is now, now that she is on the road to recovery. Jane found no comments such as that she should "snap out of" her depression, or that she was losing her mind, or that she was suffering from some mental illness. Instead, at each meeting she found people of intelligence who accepted her recovery. Members of a group also gently confront each other when the need arises, with the sole motive of helping people see themselves as others see them.

Jane accepted her powerlessness and gave it to God as she understood this newly found Power and discovered that the grace of God could do for her what she could never have done on her own.

Alcoholics Anonymous tells us: "We never apologize to anyone for depending upon our Creator. We can laugh at those who think spirituality is the way of weakness. Paradoxically, it is the way of strength. The verdict of the ages is that faith means courage. All men/women of faith have courage. They trust their God. Instead, we let God demonstrate, though us, what God can do. We ask God to remove our fear and direct our attention to what God would have us be. At once we commence to outgrow fear."

Fear is at the center of our depression, and as such has to be removed if we are to progress along our way to recovery. With courage and trust in the Higher Power you cannot fail as you continue to work this Twelve Step program. There is a saying that I think fits most of us in recovery and that is this: "The truth will set you free; but first it will make you miserable." What it means is that if you really want to start feeling better and differently we will have to confess to our need to make amends to ourselves and to others, and begin the process of choosing life over depression.

Bill W., a co-founder of *Alcoholics Anonymous*, wrote: "Our first woman Alcoholic had been a patient of Dr Harry Tiebout, and he had handed her a prepublication manuscript copy of the *Big Book*. The first reading made her rebellious, but the second convinced her. Presently she came to a meeting held in our living room, and from there she returned to the sanatorium carrying this classic message to a fellow patient. 'We aren't alone anymore.'"

No longer will anyone who has ever been treated for depression and who feels a need for understanding and ongoing support ever be alone again as long as *Depressed Anonymous* is around. It is by being part of the group that you will experience that miracle of the group which is to find that Power greater than yourself is about to restore you to a feeling of serenity and personal hope.

Step Three

Made a decision to turn our will and our lives over to the care of God, as we understood God to be.

This decision to turn our lives over to God is one of the most important we will ever make in our lives. The more we surrender to God's peace, the more we will find our way. It is the paradox of our existence that it is in the letting go that we can receive, and it is only in being in God's will - as we understand God - that we can have real life and joy. The spiritual life is not a theory. WE HAVE TO LIVE IT.

God's will is hard to determine at times – especially at such critical times as now, when we want to give up on ourselves. This is the time to give up our will and say: "God, you take it – I've had it! You do the leading now!" And you know, God will. You will begin to get more honest with yourself as you begin to look a little more closely at why you have been sad most of your life. And I might add here that for many of the members of *Depressed Anonymous*, they seem to have been depressed from the moment of their conception. Even though many people come to *Depressed Anonymous* to help them through times of significant loss in their life - such as the death of a spouse, the breakup of a relationship, the loss of a job or loss of self-esteem - many others are attempting to re-learn how to act more wisely and treat themselves kindly. Depressed people don't know how to have fun or even how to plan a pleasant activity – it's completely out of their experience. They spend most of their time berating themselves for all their real or imagined mistakes in their lives.

Depressed Anonymous helps us feel that we are beginning to have some mastery over our lives. Because of mastery over how we talk to ourselves, we find that our mood begins to change and life seems more hopeful and satisfying. One thing that we need to remember is that thoughts produce moods, moods produce feelings, and feelings produce behavior. If we can begin to think more positively about our lives and less about how bad we are, and how we no longer have to be perfect; then we will begin to feel how much happier our lives can be. We will also relearn how to trust our feelings, as we trust God more and let God thaw out our frozen feelings.

By a daily prayer and meditation time, we soon learn that the more frequent our contact is with the Higher Power, the more in touch this force will be in our lives and the more trust will you give to its leading. Once you have had more cheerful days than sad days, you will begin to see what in actuality has brought you down in the past. These sad thoughts will appear as red flags that will warn you to turn your negative thoughts to some positive picture and imagine yourself in a positive situation. You will learn how this can turn your mood around. You can change your mood by changing the way you think. Thinking causes moods which cause behavior. Meditation is likewise a waiting upon the Higher Power to reveal itself in our lives. We try daily to make conscious contact with the God of our lives as we understand God. We begin to love ourselves and each other and when we attend our meetings, we learn that it is in our openness to the Higher Power that this God of our understanding can operate. Our lives begin to assume a new hopefulness.

You are fortunate to be in *Depressed Anonymous* and can be grateful as you hear stories of people like yourself who are willing to come together and support each other in their efforts to find hope and peace.

Depressed Anonymous is a place to clean house, forgive ourselves and others, and begin to depend on God. We need to develop a God-consciousness. We learn about God from books but most importantly through our own personal experience. We experience God and the Higher Power in our group and during our personal prayer and meditation time. We come together at *Depressed Anonymous* and all our sessions begin and end with prayer. Our program is a spiritual one. We are not a religion with set dogmas and doctrines, but we are searchers of our true selves where we intend to find God and surrender our will to God. This small step can lead us to greater healing and hope.

Jim, for instance, learned that he needed more "SUNSPOTS" to bask himself in. These "SUNSPOTS" are meditation times where we can focus on all those pleasurable events, people, places or things that can make us feel happy. The trouble with most of us when we are depressed is that our whole life seems to go in to a deep pit with an eighty foot hole and an eight foot ladder.

One good way to escape from this prison is to get with a group of people who, by joining each other's section of ladder, will all eventually get to the top and out of this deep dark hole that we call depression. Think upon these small "SUNSPOTS" throughout the day and know that you are gradually coming into the light of a new day. Prepare a list of memories which at one time in your life were the cause of some joy and pleasure, and try to recreate that activity in your imagination as often as you can. At first, all you might be able to do is just make a mental decision to do it even though at the time you don't feel any particular pleasant emotion. Keep at it and with the continued encouragement of the group, you will be able to recapture a little joy and peace. You will begin to have more mastery over your life and the world and this in itself can lower your feelings of sadness. When you have a negative image or thought which produces an unpleasant feeling, replace it immediately with three positive and pleasant thoughts or mental images. In *Depressed Anonymous,* we call this "THE LAW OF THE THREES." One negative thought is immediately replaced by three pleasant thoughts and/or memories.

For the depressed person, giving up old ways of thinking and acting is much like giving up any other addiction. At first, letting go of the old behavior makes us feel uncomfortable. The old behavior wants to cling to our spirit like swamp mud hangs on to knee-high boots. Before your participation in *Depressed Anonymous,* you would go home from work, get by yourself and ruminate on how bad you felt. This new behavior will help you think differently about yourself. You will find that this Higher Power, or the God of your understanding, is not the same God that you might have met when you were young. When you were a child, you came to believe that God was watching you, ready to punish you if you were not perfect. You will begin to develop an adult new way of being related to God, as you understand God to be. With time, persistence and patience, you will gradually trust your life to this Higher Power.

One Thing the Higher Power accomplishes for any of us is the freedom of being in its will. By turning your life and will over to the Higher Power, you can make a new beginning, you get a new start, you can forgive yourself for all the times you thought you needed to be perfect, and instead accept your own self and imagine yourself the happy person you want to be. And if you attend meetings regularly and become involved, you will begin to feel better about yourself, your world and your future.

I promise you that as you continue to learn to trust others and feel accepted by them, your face will soften and you will be more relaxed knowing that you are OK. Members of the group will support you every inch of the way. Your hope will return in good measure the more you attend meetings. You will begin to feel renewed as you learn how not to be sad, how not to feel guilty and ashamed because you feel you are not like other people. Now instead of thinking about the beautiful persons, relationships or a part of the self that you may have lost, you set goals every day of how you are going to lick this depression once and for all. You have no doubt that you want to feel better and you just know that God is with you. I hope that because of your own understanding of the experience of depression and what damage it can do to people, you will now want to be used by God to reach out to others and help them regain their self-esteem and confidence. People depressed don't look on themselves too kindly.

We all believe the saying: "Motivation follows action." We all have heard it said, and we have said it ourselves: "I will do it when I feel better!" We never feel better and so we never start to change the way we feel, think and act. The feeling of helplessness remains.

The decision to begin to turn our lives and will over to the God of our understanding can only work for us as we learn to let go and let the Higher Power work its will in our lives and minds. Being in God's will is the beginning of peace and the beginning of the end of your depression with its hollowness and jitters!

We are talking about spirituality here – we are not proclaiming a religion. This is the difference of great importance. We are not subject to a book of dogmas, theological treatises or doctrine made by human beings. We are advocating a spirituality that puts God first in our lives and lets God run our lives as God sees fit. When we talk about surrendering, we get scared. How many people have I heard say: "I don't know if I want to give up my will – what will happen to me then?" This is an honest question and one that I had asked myself many times. But it was only after I hit bottom and found my depression too much for me to handle that I knew I had to give up my way of doing things, for my life couldn't get any worse. It's when we feel we can't go on with our own life that we get in touch with the waiting and loving and ever present Higher Power. It's easy to say: "I want to give up my will" - just to say the words: "I surrender" – and that's a good start, but the temptation to go back to our sadness, to sadden ourselves, is a constant one in the beginning days of our recovery.

Control is an issue which all addicts of whatever substance, emotion or relationships have to look at sooner or later in their recovery. Removing the need to be in control can only be got at by being willing to give it up to someone else – for us in *Depressed Anonymous* that means the Higher Power. When I can admit that my depression has become un-manageable, it is only at this point that I can begin to gain control over it and begin to live with hope and joy.

In *Depressed Anonymous,* we are exposed constantly to the tough message that we have to give up our self-pity and sadness if we want to be happy. We have to think in terms of what is possible with God in our lives. Sometimes people come to *Depressed Anonymous* and don't want to talk about God or the Twelve Steps, and can't understand what this has to do with how bad they feel. If after a number of meetings they still don't want to work the Twelve Steps, we recommend other groups for them. *Depressed Anonymous* is a spiritual program and it is allowing the Higher Power into our lives that eventually delivers us from the habit of feeling sad and depressed. We in *Depressed Anonymous* are committed to working the Twelve Steps and listening to each other share how God, as we understand God, has worked in our lives.

Daily we pray that God will release us from our depression and will show us God's will and way to peace. Don't give up on yourself but come back to meetings week after week. In time, the truth about yourself as revealed to you by the group and the Higher Power will set you free. That is a promise!

One of the major areas of our lives that we have a difficult time with is getting in touch with our feelings. Many of us who are presently depressed know that one of our great defenses is the denial of our feelings – our ability to feel is diminished as we continually choose numbness over vitality and spontaneity.

Jim was a member of a *Depressed Anonymous* group and he would come to each meeting and just say his name and that was that. Of course we all try to accept people where they are and when they first come to *Depressed Anonymous*, we let them know that it is OK just to sit and listen and learn from the members of the group. Everyone realizes that you never have to speak at a meeting but that you always have the right to pass and remain silent.

Jim came with a deep anger and mistrust of professionals, especially doctors, counselors and psychiatrists – whom he said were more interested in money than in helping people. Jim also felt overwhelmed by all the things he had to attend to in his life and was angry at the cards life dealt out of him.

The *Depressed Anonymous* group in their own inimitable fashion shared with him how each had found some peace and joy by making daily a good effort in working the Twelve Steps and turning their lives over to God or the Higher Power. They each expressed their own struggles and shared how coming back to the group week after week started them back on the road to recovery. They were feeling so bad that they had to trust someone with how bad they felt and so they came to the group that said it was there for depressed people. And when they started to hear how other persons were able to trust each other with their own pain, hurt, guilt and shame, it wasn't long before they progressed to the third step and were able to trust the Higher Power with their lives. The group members all expressed to Jim how they each had made a mental decision to turn their lives and their depression over to the Higher Power because they had no place to go but up. It was this surrendering to the Higher Power or God, as we understand God, that was the beginning of the overcoming of some people's addiction to the comfort of their depression. They now are willing and ready to live with some hope. In time, Jim got in touch with his anger, shared it with people who accepted it, and so was able to gradually move out of the shell that kept him from the hope that life would ever be any different for him. The depressed person just believes and takes it on faith that he/she will always be depressed and sad. Now that negative belief of being depressed forever has to be reframed and we have to tell ourselves that if we have a positive faith, our life will be better and we will begin to see changes. Many times, we get what we choose when it comes to our personal feelings.

Jim also felt that his whole problem was a chemical imbalance and that he really wasn't responsible for his plight of continual sadness. But the members of the group pointed out that any emotion, especially a negative one, will in time have certain physiological consequences which can cause the human body to get fatigued, change the appetite, cause sleep problems and promote a general feeling of helplessness. Even though antidepressants are fine for the time when they are needed to lift one's mood, one doesn't want to depend on them over any long period of time. Most doctors are sensitive to this fact and will recommend their patients to see a counselor or psychologist while the medication begins to lift the mood of the patient – they hope. Many people find that by taking some medication, they can work and function fairly normally and feel able to confront their sadness, perhaps by talking to a therapist, friend, or with their *Depressed Anonymous* group.

With any addiction to an experience, be it alcohol, eating, gambling, smoking, and for us depression, we all know that there is no "cheap grace" here in getting free of our dependency. Jim learned in time and with frequent attendance at *Depressed Anonymous* meetings, that the price of freedom from the uneasiness and hollow feelings he felt was every day to trust in the Higher Power and turn his sadness over to this God of his understanding.

Jim mentioned how he had felt anger toward members of the group at his first meeting, for what he felt was a phoniness in acting as though they were feeling better, when in reality he felt that they were putting on a show.

If there is anything a depressed person has a difficult time with, it is with someone being cheerful or happy. When we are feeling bad, we think that if we ever did smile, our face would crack. It was when Jim felt he had no place to go but up, and when his pain got greater than his own fears of himself needing help, he finally admitted to the group that his life was unmanageable and out of control. He also admitted that he had seriously thought of taking his life as he had just about lost all hope of removing this sadness which, like a cancer, was taking his life by inches. It was only when he no longer had anything to lose that he made a decision to turn his mind and his will over to the care of God, as he understood God. It was at this point that the God of his understanding or the Higher Power was allowed to work in Jim's life. God doesn't act like a gangbuster and force its way into our lives – God has to be invited. Once again, there is an invitation from us and we admit our dependence on God instead of our own addiction. It is then that our feelings begin to come alive and the flow of God's love makes its way into our lives. We begin to find that we are feeling better and that something good, even though ever so slightly, is beginning to stir within us. There is a feeling of newness that comes over us as we trust, possibly for the first time, this God who will give us our heart's desire. "God grant us the serenity to accept the things we cannot change, the courage to change the things that we can and the wisdom to know the difference." Trust God to be God, and let this Power help you, as it has helped millions of other men and women before you!

At Step Three, many of us said to our Maker, as we understood God: "God, I offer myself to Thee – to build with me and to do with me as Thou wilt. Relieve me of the bondage of self that I may better do Thy will. Take away my difficulties, that my transcendence over them may bear witness to those I would help of Thy Power, Thy love and Thy way of life. May I do Thy will always!"

Step Four

Made a searching and fearless moral inventory of ourselves.

Tom asked why we needed Step Four in our recovery. He said that he was depressed and didn't need anything else to make him feel worse – like dredging up things that he might have done in the past. Why, Tom wondered, should he resurrect old ghosts? Anyway, when we spoke about a moral inventory it reminded him of religion with its "do's" and "don'ts" with special emphasis on the "don'ts." Tom said he came into *Depressed Anonymous* to learn about what was making him depressed and that he didn't need anything else to make him feel guilty or sadder.

Some people think that for a person to dredge up old hurts and wrongs will make them that much more depressed. I guess it depends on what types of stuff we put on our inventory. The following list of defects of character can help our sadness persist: our perfectionism, our need to control, our fears, guilt, shame or resentments, dishonesty, selfishness, passivity, anger, indecisiveness, fear of change or finally the inability to live with uncertainty. When we begin to ask God for help in removing these areas from our life, this asking for help will not make us more depressed – it will in fact make us more hopeful. In Step Three we said we make a decision. This means just that and not just a promise as it says in the *Alcoholics Anonymous Big Book*. When we begin to surrender our will and our life to the Higher Power and are willing to expose our defects to others in the group, it is then that our life may be able to take on a peace coupled with new purpose. This really is an essential and necessary step that has to be taken if we want to leave our prison of depression behind. We must not only make a searching inventory of how we view ourselves, our world and our future, but we must also take stock of any character defects that keep us locked into personal feelings of shame and guilt. We need to look at the areas that Dorothy Rowe has identified in her book *Depression: The Way Out of our Prison* where she lists the six major beliefs of persons who get themselves depressed. All depressed people hold all these beliefs in one degree or another. She contends that most depressed people hold these facts about themselves immutable truths, unchanging and set in granite. They think nothing will ever change in their lives. These beliefs become the sort of material that we need to list if we are to get free of the depression that has played such a big role in our lives.

The first immutable belief, according to Dorothy Rowe, that many depressed hold onto, like the inspired words from God, is the belief that no matter how good and nice I appear to be, I am really bad, evil, valueless, and unacceptable to myself and to others.

Step Four is a critical step if we want to begin the journey toward wholeness, peace and having good feelings about ourselves again. But if we want to stay in the pit of sadness then the belief that we are worthless and not quite good enough will definitely limit our awareness of what we can become and what we can do for ourselves. I believe a lot of our difficulties have their roots in our need to be perfect and to do things the way others expect. It's as though we have to take care of their needs before our own. Significant persons from our past have promoted the belief that for me to be acceptable I had to do things their way and their way alone. I had to please them or I might be abandoned and left alone forever. This in itself is a frightening situation for any of us. I needed continually to attempt to be someone other than myself. I constantly was filled with sadness, as I never felt I could measure up to what others wanted me to do or be. My whole life was graded on what others thought I should be. Good was never good enough and so I continued to test the limits in an effort to excel but the limits were never clearly marked out. I sensed that somehow I couldn't ever measure up to others' expectations and that made me feel ashamed of myself. Not only did I feel guilt but I also felt ashamed – ashamed that my inadequacies would be exposed for everyone to see and ridicule. My constant fear was that others would see how bad I really was.

This is how the inventory can help us unearth and eradicate those character defects as we begin to see the truth manifest itself as we take stock of our lives. We need to learn how to give ourselves the good breaks that we would give any other human begin instead of our self-bashing. Any compliment given to us we immediately deny and act as if it doesn't really apply – especially, we think, if people knew the real me. We continually perpetuate the belief that we are no good and worthless, because of past childhood beliefs still unconsciously influence our present thoughts and behavior. These past events, some not even consciously remembered, are somehow still driving the sadness in our daily lives. This vague feeling of beginning a mistake and feeling that we are just tolerated by others is a belief that must be dismantled and thrown on the junk heap if we are to be happy persons that we are meant to be. We are mourning part of ourselves that was never able to be given expression and this makes us sad. When we bring up this fact at our meetings we hear how others in the group likewise had no childhood and that the ability to have fun was terribly missing in our youngest years. Spontaneity and a childlike frivolity were considered out of place in many of our homes. Children were not allowed to talk about their feelings or even to trust. All of this put us at risk for depression as we swallowed feelings that we weren't allowed to express.

We need to get down on paper our feelings about ourselves and locate where we got our first impressions of ourselves. What type of attitudes did we grow up within our homes regarding our parents and siblings? Were there family secrets that weren't allowed to be talked about outside our homes? Did we ever see our parents showing affection for one another? Did we frequently observe our parents fighting? Did we fear as youngsters that Mom and Dad might abandon us and that we might end up being orphans? If our parents did divorce, did we blame ourselves for their divorce? It is precisely in doing the inventory that we can bring out our feelings of shame and early feelings of embarrassment because of how these significant persons from childhood made us feel about ourselves.

I still remember feeling embarrassed when my third grade teacher told me in front of the whole class that I would never be like my brother who was much smarter than me. I used to feel my face get hot every time I thought about that embarrassing incident. But the more I share my shame of having been exposed to others about something that I had no control over, the freer I become of that fear. The same principle is at work here in the *Depressed Anonymous* group. We can take our own personal inventory of our weaknesses and fears and trust the group to hear us out and accept our stories of shame and hurt as we accept theirs. We begin to see how and why so many people feel bad because in their earlier years people made them feel that they could never measure up to the way others expected them to grow up. By becoming our little child once more, we paradoxically grow up.

We have made the decision to turn our will and our lives over to the care of the God of our understanding and this in itself will help us to get honest within ourselves and with members of the group. This honesty will set us free as we pull ourselves away from the old self that we once were and begin to be in touch with our deepest and truest selves. Our exhaustive and honest search into ourselves will begin to reveal to us that so much of what we thought to be evil or worthless in our earlier lives was a scaffold built on sand. Character is built by truth and the willingness to list the truths in ourselves. It can be a painful search but it will reveal that it's all right to be imperfect and not to have all the answers. It's all right to trust others with our deepest fears and hurts, and to know that we can still be loved and respected even though we share how bad and evil we have considered ourselves over the years. It will be evident in time that one's feelings of deep sadness did not come out of nowhere but indeed was the result of the way we were led to believe and think about ourselves.

"To thine own self first be true" is an old axiom that has much merit for those of us who work the spiritual program of the Twelve Steps. Often in therapy I ask people to list as many strengths as they can, and for some this is a difficult task when they are depressed and the world appears to be a grey and fearsome dark place. But this is the inventory that we must make – we must begin to look at our strengths and stop wallowing in the self-pity which denies the new directions and progress occurring in our lives through the love of our depression; namely that we can't seem to see the gracious goodness in ourselves that has been placed there for all time by the Higher Power. This in itself is the attitude that keeps alive our depression; sadness and self-deprecating attitudes. We need to look at our assets and list our strengths as we gather together time after time in our *Depressed Anonymous* group or in our individual working of the Twelve Step program in our lives. We likewise need to remove as quickly as possible all the old excuses and reasons that we cling to and that keep us depressed and out of healthful recovery. Let's be objective about ourselves and admit that just as we have caused ourselves to be depressed, we likewise can un-depress ourselves in the same way.

We are not here to condemn ourselves, but to evaluate how we can achieve an inner peace and serenity that is promised to those who let go to trust in their Higher Power, or the God of their understanding. It won't do all that good to try to search out the why of our depression. What what must be discovered is the how to begin to reverse this sad state of affairs in our lives now. Our family and teachers and our unhappy experiences taught us to believe that we were bad and valueless, but we are free to change that belief. We must realize that we are responsible for the way we feel and that we can't blame it on our childhood, parents, significant others or the weather. We must take responsibility for the way we believe. It is without doubt that the more we being to talk to ourselves in a positive way and regular way the more we are able to develop the habit of acting in a consistently positive life-giving way. First of all we must motivate ourselves to some type of action if we are to emerge successfully from our continued state of sadness and lethargy.

The second immutable truth, according to Dorothy Rowe, is that "Other people are such that I must fear, hate and envy them." If we believe that we are bad and valueless, then it follows that we must fear other people because they can find out how bad we are and reject us. When we fear anyone for long enough we come to hate that person, and when we fear someone, we don't get close enough to that person to see his difficulties. We think he is having an easy time, and so we envy him. So you will believe that everyone around you is an enemy. It's most difficult to learn to live in trust if you are in a constant state of terror of those around you. We need to look at all our relationships and seek out the people for whom we presently have strong feelings of hate, envy and fear. We have to root out of ourselves all those strong emotions which are like bars of steel keeping us locked up in these emotions of powerlessness. It is only when we are able to look honestly into our souls that we will begin to see that it is how we feel about others that has a present influence on our feelings, and whenever we need to feel back in control we immediately drop back into a sad feeling – it keeps us from having to feel too much. We are much like the practicing alcoholic taking one more drink to medicate and numb unpleasant feelings.

Sadness is likewise an addiction in that it is used to blunt a very painful loss, a thought of a future loss or to numb the way our world happens to be experienced by us today. We would do well to track the times that we become sad as well as track the automatic thoughts that continually throw us into a state of despair. It's very much like the nicotine addiction where the smoking addict who is trying to stop smoking keeps track of where, when and how many cigarettes he/she smokes a day. He or she keeps an inventory of the difference it makes when engaged in different activities. Do some people, places or things cause him/her to smoke more or less? All this can help list problem areas, the areas that are filled with stress which cause him/her to experience some relief from the pain. So, we need to look more closely at the times we sink ourselves back into the pit of depression.

We also might find that our self-confidence has greatly diminished since we have been depressed and so we need to realize that if we are able to regain any skills in relating to others then we must get out of our little circle of life and get involved with others like ourselves in a *Depressed Anonymous* group. We also need to realize that this Step Four is only for ourselves. It would be comfortable to sit back and blame others for the way our lives have turned out – but only we can make the inventory. Take responsibility for ourselves and admit that we are the cause of how we feel. It's at this point that we claim responsibility for self and can honestly say that our inventory is a searching and fearless one.

Denial, projection and rationalization are major defense mechanisms of those persons who are saddening themselves. Over the years they have denied that their behavior is abnormal or that they have any control over the way they feel. Also, people who are addicted to sadness in their lives may have projected onto someone else the blame for the way they have felt all these years. They also tend to rationalize that since someone hurt them in the past they have the right to sadden themselves today. When we interact with people who have tried to understand themselves and their need for such defenses, we can come to understand the way we use these defenses and then give up our dependence on them.

Being socially isolated is a key component in most people's depression. The fact that many depressed people prefer to sit and stew in their isolation and pain precludes their feeling better. It is only when we can get past the blaming of others; the denying of our own ability to choose a healthier way to live and think that our depression will wither away for lack of attention. But making the decision to turn our wills and our lives over to the care of the God of our understanding is the beginning of the end for our depressing lifestyle. The self-help group of *Depressed Anonymous* makes it possible, if you choose to find men and women to whom you need not apologize for your depression. You will not be judged for it.

A clear light seems to fall upon us all – when we open our eyes. Since our blindness is caused by our own defects, we must first deeply realize what they are. Constructive meditation is the first requirement for each new step in our spiritual growth.

Step Five

Admitted to God, to ourselves and to another human being the exact nature of our wrongs.

Mary couldn't understand how this Step Five had anything to do with her. She hadn't done anything wrong to anybody. She was coming to *Depressed Anonymous* to find a way out of the sadness which always seemed to play a large part of her life.

She did know that her parents were practicing alcoholics, and she lived in constant terror as a child because of their constant bickering and fighting when they were drunk. Because of shame, Mary was never able to share her story with any of her friends. In time, she began to think that her feelings were disloyal to her parents, whom she felt she had to love because they were her parents. She said she got confused because they seemed to want her around sometimes, but at other times they told her what a worthless and lazy girl she was. The first thing that hurt most, she said, is that she believed them. So now she wonders how this Fifth Step applies to her when it's her parents who need to admit their wrongs to her. Mary was puzzled. All she wanted to do was to get over some of the anger that she still held for the way her parents neglected her when she was growing up. She said that every time she went back home, a sadness seemed to just come over her, as though out of the blue, and for no apparent reason. She also said that her stomach got all knotted up.

Everyone who works the program, like Mary, is very much aware that if they want peace and serenity, then they have to continue this search into themselves. The only condition for those who want to join the *Depressed Anonymous* group is a sincere desire to stop saddening themselves. As Mary learned from the other members of *Depressed Anonymous,* it wasn't until she could let out her feelings of anger and rage, a little at a time, that she began to feel better.

The Fifth Step is usually done with another member of the *Depressed Anonymous* group or any other person who is working the Twelve

Step program in their own life. When you want to start cleaning house and stop blaming others for the way you feel, and take responsibility for yourself, then you know that you are in earnest about beginning your program.

There is a saying that "When a ship is in a storm and in danger, dump the cargo, and save the ship." You have been brought to a point in your life, be it a young life or an older life, where you can begin to dump some of the garbage of your past. It is in working the Twelve Steps – inch by inch getting better. The freedom that you feel is marvelous as you begin to see that there is a light at the end of the tunnel. There is hope and it feels good.

In *Depression: The Way Out Of Your Prison*, Dorothy Rowe lists the third immutable belief as: "Life is terrible and death is worse." Many depressed persons find themselves in this bind. You are on the horns of a dilemma – you feel that you can't ever win and you see no way out of this everlasting sadness, and so you get used to your sad thoughts and continue to isolate yourself from the real world and others. If you want to free yourself from the horns of this dilemma, you have to ask yourself, as well as members of the group what it is that makes you feel that life is so terrible and sad.

So many times it is our perfectionism that makes life so difficult and we never seem able to meet the challenge of our own unrealistic goals and ambitions. We never can do it quite well enough. We need to be able to trust that we can make mistakes. In my past, it has not been permissible to do that. It is this continual search for ways to be perfect that drives us back to sadness and the misery of our addiction. We believe that we will never have a respite from the pain of our loneliness, and that the hell of our existence can only be relieved by numbing our sensitive feelings.

We do this by withdrawing contact from others. We often need to admit to God and others that we love to play the martyr role and have others tell us what a "saint" we are for all the awful things that we have had to put up with for so many years. This is what we want to hear. At least someone knows the hell we've been through. As a martyr, we are waiting to be rewarded for our goodness. Once we give up this idea, we know not only in our head, but also in our heart that this totally accepting Higher Power to which we surrender is always ready to accept us as we are – not as we think we should be.

For many of us, it's our own sense of worthlessness that we need to look at and admit to God, another human being and ourselves that this self-pity and low self-esteem are not what God wants us to experience. It is relatively easy to tell God some of the garbage that is part of the burden that we carry around but the big job is to admit to another person our feelings, faults and weaknesses. Really to get something out of Step Five, you must share your pain with another person. It is in the sharing of our sins and wrongs that gradually we are freed from the shame, guilt and fear that keep us in the prison of our depression.

How many excuses we can think up to prevent us from going to friends to tell them the exact nature of our wrong? We can think of so many reasons why we can't tell others why we are the way we are. For many of us who need to be perfect, we have a difficult time telling someone else that we might not be what we appear to be.

We must see ourselves as we really are. If we are ever sad about people we have hurt, or even more so angry about people who have hurt us over the years, then we need to get this out in the open. We also need to share the anger inside us that has been swallowed for so many years and which likewise needs to be expressed. We need to get in touch with the feelings of rage that have been under our tight control over the years. So many times we have felt that if we ever let go of our rage it would fling us completely out of control and we would experience complete annihilation. What we need to discover is that whatever emotion we express – anger, tears, laughter – does not go on forever, but comes naturally to an end.

The fourth immutable belief that the depressed person has is that since bad things happened in the past, only bad things will happen in the future. This belief that rules so many of our lives seems such an accurate fact - we can't ever trust the fact that we might feel good again. In fact, our misery is such a predictable part of our lives that we are afraid to step out and think differently or live with any amount of hope, because this new happy feeling won't last anyway. How many times have I heard people who have been depressed for as many years as they can remember not want to give up and let go of the feeling that makes them miserable. They would rather stay mired down in the pain of their sadness than risk the chance in the sunlight of hope and serenity. I can understand how people would be afraid of trusting God to let them feel hope and peace because all they have known is the pain of their depression – but at the same time, I believed others in the group who tell us how they took the risk to turn their minds and wills over to the care of God, and how their trust, as small as a mustard seed, began to bring them out of their sadness and despair. You have to be brutally honest with yourself and really want to escape from depression. You do this by admitting your own need to be depressed and your own fear of the alternative, namely taking charge of your life and assuming full responsibility for the way you think, feel and behave. It's much safer to remain depressed.

Many times we hear how depression is anger turned inward. This is one way o explain it. Depression is also a way to keep from assuming our rightful place in the world and society. You must tell others that your very fear of the future of others is the very thing that builds your prison. You need to surrender the fears and hurts of your life. You need to give them up to the Higher Power or to God, as you understand God. It is with this in mind that you begin to gain more insights and honesty in your life. Others in the DA group will also help you see that you can blame the other people in your life for your problems all you want, but it is only when you no longer see yourself as the victim that you can stand up and say that you no longer choose to stay depressed. "I am going to enjoy life and hope for good things to begin to happen to me," you can say. I think sometimes we must confess that we liked being called "depressive" as it made us feel as though we couldn't help being the way we were, and of course we know this isn't true. Once we admit our victim stance and no longer consider ourselves as permanent sufferers of depression, then this honesty can release a new sense of identity for ourselves. The support of the group will also allow us to say: "I don't have to be what I was anymore. I don't need it!"

The fifth immutable belief that builds hopelessness in us is the belief that it is wrong to get angry. We have learned from childhood that not only do little girls not show anger, but little boys likewise were made to believe that any type of outward expression of emotion or anger is a sign that you are out of control, and being out of control is bad. But if anything can cause us to be depressed, it is a lifetime of swallowing our anger. This might have its roots in our childhood when we were abused physically, emotionally, or even sexually by a parent, relative or guardian. The mere thought of this might throw us into a deep sense of personal worthlessness and rage until we are able to get in touch with it. Sometimes this rage is so powerful that we have to numb ourselves so as not to feel the power of it and so be afraid that it will destroy our very selves.

We don't advocate that you come to *Depressed Anonymous* meetings and take your anger out on anybody there, but we do advocate that persons begin to allow themselves to feel this anger inside them and when they do, they will soon talk about some of these feelings that might for some go back a long time. Again, it is my experience that the people who come and stay with *Depressed Anonymous* are those who have been depressing most of their lives. Now, by their active participation in the program, they have discovered a group of men and women who speak the same language and who are helping others learn how to leave their depression if they so choose. But when we are angry, we need to say that we are angry about this or that person, this or that experience, and then feel it. Don't run from it or act as though it's not there, but get in touch with the feeling and see what it's saying to you, now. You won't die from feeling it – you will be more by feeling it.

Some people have found that just saying to another person that they have done something they are ashamed of can in itself help them find a new acceptance of themselves that they have never felt before. A good Fifth Step covers all the major areas of our lives that we need to look at and for which we ask God's forgiveness. A good way to start is to be willing to make a list of all the major wrongs in our life and then take these to a trusted friend, and tell him/her the exact nature of our wrongs.

The sixth immutable belief that you must hold to if you want to stay depressed is that you must never forgive anyone, least of all yourself. This is a sure fire way to make certain that you stay depressed. Most persons who stay depressed are experts at this one and know that they are so bad that no one can ever forgive them for all the bad things they have done in the past. Of course, the depressed people realize after a number of *Depressed Anonymous* meetings that they have a tendency to make mountains out of molehills and so any little thing that they have done wrong is ruminated upon time and again until they have taken the role of judge and executioner of their very own selves. They turn their mistakes, sins and inadequacies over and over again in their minds until that is all they can think of. This is the nature of an addiction; the compulsion to repeat becomes habit.

It is this attitude of unforgiveness that freezes the depressed person's life in the past tense and forces him/her to live in the painful past of pain and pressure of real or imagined sins. The depressed person can't believe that all things are forgivable.

I think that many depressed people need to admit that they are harder on themselves than anyone else would be. I'm sure that if they heard someone else tell of a situation the same as theirs, the depressed person would be the first one to show and extend them forgiveness and compassion. Depression feeds on hurt, pain and self-doubt. When we are depressed, we have a need to bash ourselves for our imagined crimes and sinfulness. The Fifth Step, if done genuinely and prayerfully, will in time help restore our sense of freedom and belief that we are truly forgiven. It is the miracle of the group and its acceptance, love and nurture that helps the depressed person feel secure without recourse to depression.

Many times, persons who come to *Depressed Anonymous* come because of a broken marriage, loss of love, loss of a job, or because of one's self-esteem. People tell members of the group that they have never respected themselves, their own intuitions, or anything else that was good in themselves. If they stay with the program, they will have to admit that they have ignored their good points and remained afraid and penned up in the isolation of their feelings of worthlessness. This is where the depressed need to start their checklist and admit that they have seen themselves as bad and unacceptable; that they have envied and erred others; that they thought life was terrible and death was worse; that only bad things could happen to them in the future because only bad things had happened to them in the past; that they didn't allow themselves to express emotions; and that they never forgave themselves or anyone else. One's personal recovery begins by telling the God of our understanding that we surrender all these defects of character and that because of them, our lives have been un-manageable. Our recovery begins the minute we make the decision to turn our minds and our wills over to the care of God, as we understand God.

By our continual shutting ourselves up in the little world of our own mind, we gradually sink more and more into despair and feel that no one can understand how we think and feel. The biggest freedom that we can gain from confessing to someone else is that we no longer have to have it all together and be perfect. We can begin to admit it when we are petty, selfish and self-centered. We can then admit that we want to have restored a sense of peace by getting free from all worry and fear from the past and by turning these over to the Higher Power. We can then discover that forgiving ourselves and being forgiven by God are one in the same thing. The group will see to it that the more you admit your own fears about yourself and the future, the less terror the present will hold for you.

Alcoholics Anonymous has found that. "When we decide who is to hear our story, we waste no time. We have a written inventory and we are prepared for a long talk. We explain to our partner what we are about to do and why we have to do it. We pocket our pride and go to it, illuminating every twist of character, every dark cranny of the past. Once we have taken this step, withholding nothing, we are delighted. We can look the world in the eye. We can be alone at perfect peace and ease. Our fears fall from us. We begin to feel the nearness of our Creator. We may have had certain spiritual beliefs, but now we begin to have a spiritual experience. . ."

My dear friends, it is this spiritual experience, to feel that God is with you, and that this joy is the joy that will restore your youth and renew your spirit. We no longer have to be the way we are – we can choose to feel and be different. Others are doing it – so can you!

Step Six

Were entirely ready to have God remove all these defects of character.

There is a list of seven character defects that have been traditionally called the seven deadly sins. Even though the total list is not familiar to many of us, most have been experienced by all of us at one time or another in our life. The seven deadly sins are pride, laziness, gluttony, envy/jealousy, greed, lust and dishonesty.

When we realize that we are going to let the God of our understanding remove the defect of our character it is clear that we have to let go and let God do its work in our lives. We are saying that we are going to allow God to remove those defects of character that keep pulling us back into the experience of depression. We know that our depression is what keeps us from other people as well as keeping our feelings frozen and out of touch with our real selves. The First Five steps have brought us to this point where we now admit to someone else and to God the exact nature of our wrings. We have made a confession and come right. We revealed our secrets to some other human and this released in us a freedom never before felt, until we were ready to have God remove our defects. By our admission that we aren't perfect and that our lives have been out of control we can begin to get our problems out into the light of day. By trusting others with our deepest hurts and fear, this sometimes can reduce the size of these very same obstacles to happiness. We might also have felt God's presence for the first time as we began to experience a new sense of peace living inside of us.

When we look back, we realize that the things which came to us when we put ourselves in God's hands were better than anything we could have planned.

It is now that we need the strength of humility to face ourselves and declare that we are a broken and hurting individual, and that our addiction to depression has kept us from really living and trusting in God or the Higher

Power. Once we have dug out in Steps Four and Five what has been the cause of our chronic descent into hopelessness, we can not only seek out the solution to our patterns of dysfunction but can now list our strengths. We need to begin to identify our positive strengths and depend on them if we are to move towards hope and a sense of mastery over our lives. Many people, for a lot of reasons, are blind to the fact that they are addicted to depression, and continue to live in a state of denial and rationalization about their need to sadden themselves. They are saddicts.

Saddicts believe that it is much better to choose to live in a state of misery than to choose to live in a state of serenity by letting God remove their defects of character. So many people choose the predictableness of misery to the risky feeling of being unsure and scared over the new and faint feelings of lightness and cheer. As the depressed person gradually beings to tear down the wall of his or her denial that he or she is addicted to sadness whenever life gets stressful, this in itself is the starting point in the recovery process. Most of us tend to avoid the unfamiliar and stay with with what they know. We are like the practicing alcoholic who, whenever he/she meets a stressful or unpleasant person, place or memory, starts to medicate themselves with alcohol. The overeater, gambler, smoker, sexual addict are all driven by their compulsions. The emptiness of our lives is like a hole that continually needs to be filled with some compulsive and addictive behavior. By letting go of our excessive tightfisted hold on our life, which paradoxically in itself causes us to lose hold, we start to face reality for the first time without the crippling crutch of our compulsion. We let go of our compulsion to repeat the ritual of addictions.

Bill W., speaking of his own depression, states that: "My depression deepened unbearably, and finally it seemed to me as though I were at the very bottom of the pit. For the moment, the last vestige of my proud obstinacy was crushed. All at once I found myself crying out: "If there is a God, let Him show Himself! I am ready to do anything, anything!" Suddenly the room lit up with great white light. It seemed to me, in the mind's eye, that I was on a mountain and that a wind, not of air but of spirit, was blowing. And then it burst upon me that I was a free man. Slowly the ecstasy subsided. I lay on the bed, but now for a time I was in another world, a new world of consciousness. All about me and through me there was a wonderful feeling of Presence, and I thought to myself: "So this is the God of the preachers!"

It takes getting to a point where all we can do is surrender and let go of our own will and let God be in charge of our lives. In the case of Bill W., one of the founders of *Alcoholics Anonymous*, he pleaded to God for help and admitted that he was ready to do anything, anything to get relief. This uncovering of what God wants for us will help us see how we need to change the way we act, feel and think. I have heard many say that they would love to get rid of their depression, meaning they would no longer depress themselves if they could be sure that there wouldn't be any more pain. Of course, you and I know that this can't be possible. Bill W. stated that pain is the touchstone of spiritual progress.

A character defect is something that we all suffer from and it is in working the Twelve Step program that we discover how to overcome these defects. Normally as an addictive personality, as we have mentioned before, we have a hole deep inside of us that we try to fill with food, alcohol, gambling, sex, love, depression etc. Paradoxically, the continued feeding of our compulsion makes the hole that much deeper. The more we want to experience the temporary comfort of the addiction the more that experience dictates the course of our life's focus. Our whole attention is directed towards getting more of the comforting experience. I am sure that not too many people would think that their lifelong experience with depression was an addiction but I am telling you that it is just that.

I see it as a character defect to continue to choose the chronic state of depression when you could feel hopeful like others who are working the Twelve Steps and who are trusting the Higher Power to take away their fears, obsessions, and anxieties that they hold for themselves.

According to the medieval church, pride was the deadliest of the seven deadly sins because it stopped people from changing. It is my pride which keeps me from admitting that I am the reason for my own depression. We need the humility to say to God and the group that my life is definitely un- manageable and that it is only the belief in God or the Higher Power that can enable me to move out of this depression.

In this step, as in the Fourth and Fifth Steps, we continue to write out and describe the different character defects that we feel might have got us into trouble along life's way. We began to drop out of life and began to sit back and watch the world go by. We became aware that we weren't having fun anymore – if we ever did – and we began to ruminate on how awful we are and how everyone must think we are the worst person ever. Again we need to look at how we see ourselves and admit that we aren't perfect and that's OK. It's the need to be perfect that keeps us anxious, fearful and helpless. We will realize that we can just be us and that we don't have to live up to anyone else's expectations beside our own.

That we are entirely ready to have God remove our defects of character says that we are no longer going to resist making changes in our life and that we want God to start the work of making us a new creation. This work of having our defects removed takes time – and for most people, a lifetime. The idea is at least to get started and realize that the more you become conscious of areas in your life that need to be looked at, the Higher Power will help you see where you need to put your attention. Very deep, sometimes quite forgotten, damaging emotional conflicts persist below the level of consciousness. At the time of these occurrences, they may have given our emotions violent twists which have since discolored our personalities and altered our lives for the worse. This is why it is so important to talk with others in your own family about origins and about those significant people who cared for you when you were a child.

To have lost a parent early in life, either through death or divorce, can have a serious effect on the life of a young child. Early losses in life cause a lot of hurt later on in life and many people think that their depression just happens, out of the blue without rhyme or reason. But usually there is a reason, and most probably it is buried deep in the unconscious because it has been too painful to look at. It is in sharing with a trusted friend, group member(s) or therapist that you can gradually let out the bits of secret that has been under lock for years. It is also when we can be in contact with persons we trust that the hurts of the past can be revealed.

Now that you have admitted that depression has left you feeling helpless and in its grip, you can begin to see how guilt, a sense of shame and losses throughout earlier life might have predisposed one to a depression that now has become a way of life, with the comfort and excuse for not living life to the full!

I think this might be a major stumbling block for many people who come to *Depressed Anonymous* when they hear that they have character defects. For instance, what does all this have to do with their depression? For many people there might be a tendency not to talk about how they hurt, and how they can't allow themselves to grieve life's losses, such as persons whom they love and have lost, a lost job or a childhood that they have never had. For some, retirement can have a crippling effect. Many people that are depressed feel helpless and have no one who understands their situation. At present, in the depth of their depression, they can't begin to think that they might have caused their depression themselves, because the onslaught has been slow and imperceptible. They feel they are going crazy and losing their minds. They feel they can't get another thought into their brain. They also forget easily and can't seem to concentrate much on anything. They also bash themselves unmercifully for all the evil things that they have done. They fear the exposure of their crimes, as they would like to call them, and continue to ruminate on how bad they must be. By pushing down any hopeful or light feelings and preventing them ever coming to the surface of their mind, they push down all feelings. When you push down one feeling, you push them all down. We are not dealing with keys on a piano, where one key being depressed has no effect on the one next to it.

It is only when the pain is greater than the fear of talking to someone about their depression that progress begins. Then inability to seek help, coupled with how hopeless and dark everything is, makes it quite difficult for the depressed person to come out from his or her darkened world into the light. It is the light of self-love that begins to shine when more revelations are made to someone else about one's sadness and despair and changes begin to occur. When it begins to register in our minds that it is in surrendering that we win, it is then that our lives take on a new turn. We are ready to move forward when we submit to the Higher Power's light operating in our hearts and lives. When we are "entirely ready" means that there will be full fledged effort on our part to have God assist us in getting through this depression. We have to give this our best. We can't let ourselves be fooled into thinking that we got our depression the same way that someone would get the flu or catch a cold. We know that somewhere along the path of life we have overloaded the circuits and have felt overwhelmed by a sense of responsibility, guilt or shame. And that this has produced the chronic depression that we can't seem to shake off.

The *Depressed Anonymous* program based on the Twelve Steps is a spiritual program, and one in which you and I continually try to better ourselves and hold off the temptation to depress ourselves when this or that stressful situation, person or memory pushes its way into our minds. It is then that you have to go to the Serenity Prayer and also turn to the Higher Power and tell it that you are not going to depend on a mood of sadness any more but that you are going to depend on it, the Higher Power, to get you through this moment, this hour and this day. You will live one day at a time and stay out of tomorrow, where the anxiety and fear lie, and out of yesterday, where hurt and anger live. This is the only place that we really can be, namely, in today, in the moment, in this hour!

For many of us, our fear of others and our need to avoid situations has caused us deep psychic pain and confusion. Any time we feel the need to get off to the quiet and think sad thoughts, we become acutely aware that we are not going to do anything hopeful for ourselves. Instead we ask the Higher Power to remove these addictive thoughts and behavior and grant us the serenity, the will and the courage to look positively to Godly strength, power, and will in our personal lives.

Most times when people hear about surrendering their lives to the Higher Power or turning their wills over to the God of their understanding, they find this invitation a most difficult one. So many times people fear that God will have them do something that will cause them pain or that will make their lives unbearable.

As we have said, Steps Four and Five have helped us to uncover our defects and now we are in a position, with the support of the group, to focus in on how certain defects of character have caused us to lose serenity and peace of mind and heart, and have caused us to stay imprisoned in our world of sad and negative thoughts and feelings.

In the meetings we hear the positive stories of those members who share with us how their lives were before *Depressed Anonymous.* So many people who were depressed had not taken care of themselves physically or spiritually, and had no close friend with whom to confide their hurts and the storm going on inside themselves. So often it is the person who seems to have lost any meaning for his or her life who is now struggling to find their true self. The recovering members of the *Depressed Anonymous* group continually tell us that they are entirely ready to have their defects of character removed. While accepting God and the group into their lives, their personal letting go has enabled them to experience the presence and peace of God.

We have emphasized willingness as being indispensable. Are we now ready to let God remove from us all the things which we have admitted are objectionable? Can God take them all – every one? If we still cling to something we will not let go. We ask God to help us to be willing. When ready, we say something like this: "My Creator, I am now willing that you should have all of me, good and bad. I pray that you now remove from me every single defect of character which stands in the way of my usefulness to you and my fellows. Grant me strength, as I go out from here, to do your bidding. Amen!"

We know that our willpower alone can't get us out of this prison of depression, but only a belief in a force or power greater than ourselves. So by working Step Six we continue to be in God's will and let God help us discover and root out those defects of character that keep us prisoner.

Lack of power that was our dilemma. We had to find a power by which we could live, and it had to be a Power greater than ourselves.

Step Seven

Humbly asked God to remove our shortcomings.

We can never really recover from our addictions and find serenity unless we start to practice some humility. Humility is the bottom line if we are to leave our depression. We must ask that our shortcomings be removed if we are to get beyond our hurting ourselves into the self that we want to become.

We know that the English word: "humility" comes from the Latin word: "humus," which means earth. If we are honest and humble, we then will be true to ourselves and to others. We will no longer continue to deny the facts about our addiction to sadness and tell ourselves that the only thing that we need to do is just take some pills and we'll be all right. Pills are fine to take away the pain, and we are thankful that they are there because we need them to help us get back on our feet. But pills cannot remove the reason for the pain, nor can they remove our shortcomings. We have to face the truth and admit that somehow I am the cause of my depression. And by our contact with others who are also depressed, we can determine some better strategies on how to get through our depression. We can now work on brushing aside any stigma attached to our depression, and admit that right now we are helpless, like the alcoholic who comes to *Alcoholics Anonymous* and said that he had tried every other method of freeing himself from his compulsive behavior and was now willing to try this Twelve Step program. This program of recovery has worked for millions who are sober today and who are taking their message of how it was with their life before they began to live and work with the Twelve Step program. They, like all members of Twelve Step programs, who are serious about their recovery, can tell people how their lives have changed since they have begun to live the steps.

We learn with time that it is only by spring cleaning and admitting our powerlessness that we begin to recover. Now that I humbly admit my shortcomings, the Higher Power can begin to work in my life. Without a doubt, it is when we don't want to go to our *Depressed Anonymous* meetings that we really need to be there. It is easy to sit at home and reflect on how bad we are and how bleak and uninviting our future appears to be. But when we become more humble (truthful) and share how we have surrendered our need to be perfect and now can face the truth about ourselves – it is then that we can begin to live.

We notice in Step Seven that we don't tell God how we want God to remove our shortcomings – we leave that up to God. This of course takes time, just as it took time to develop our shortcomings and our defects of character. Sometimes, we hear some professionals say that people who are depressing themselves shouldn't spend time taking an inventory of their faults or shortcomings because that is what got us here in the first place – namely, dissecting and bashing ourselves for all the bad things we have done and have become. Why would those depressed want to make themselves sadder? The answer to this is that you will not make yourself sadder; you will make yourself healthier as you humbly admit how you have kept yourself locked up in prison of your depression by any or all of the following; your perfectionism, your anger, anxiety, indecisiveness, feeling always overwhelmed, self-doubts, all or nothing thinking, your passivity and avoidance of getting in touch with your feelings, people pleasing, pessimism towards yourself, lack of feeling competent, loss of identity, feeling unconnected to the world, and finally, feeling socially isolated. These are some of the shortcomings that each of us has to look at if we are to live with any amount of freedom. Some of the above are sure to be part of the depressed person's life and thinking.

As one person told Dorothy Rowe: "When I think of all those years I wasted being depressed, I wish I would have listened. I wish I'd realized that all I had to do was to say I'd had enough of being put upon and put down, feeling that there was something wrong with me. I'd like to go up to the hospital and tell everybody: 'You don't have to be like this.' Up there nobody ever told me that. I'd see those people going on and on being miserable. If I'd have seen someone like me now, it would have given me hope."

In the group, as well as in our own individual times of reflection, we admit that perfectionism has affected our belief system, which in turn affects the way we feel, with the result that our behavior acts this belief out in that never ending cycling and downward feeling of defeat.

We who tend to be perfectionists experience anxiety and/or panic attacks, fearing some vague punishment if we don't produce up to our unrealistic expectations. The perfectionist feels unaccepted by others and himself/herself.

Sometimes the physical symptoms accompanying perfectionism are stomach problems, overeating and an inability to get to sleep. It's obvious that thinking these perfectionist thoughts doesn't do us any good. Fatigue is another indicator that something is being overdone and out of whack in our life.

We need humbly to ask God to remove this major shortcoming of needing to be perfect, because we will never be able to accept ourselves unless we admit that we are made of clay like everyone else. No one expects you or me to be some superior human being. Somewhere along in our development, most likely in our early childhood, we got the message that we weren't OK unless we did everything just perfect. We want to admit the need to be perfect to God and to another human being. We have to tell ourselves that it is OK to fail and to make mistakes. No longer will we accept our past thinking that our worth is based on our ability to produce. This is erroneous thinking!

One makes a choice when making a decision. One of the hard things in a depressed person's life is making a decision. The indecision is what really gets to a person and continually helps him or her remain off balance. Usually this indecision is the result of an emotional war going on inside, and both sides war over who will have their way. The more depressed we become, the less able we are able to muster up the necessary energy to make a decision that will benefit us. I believe that this moral type of inventory is not going to be detrimental to our recovery because it is all about our recovery. We are not intending for it to make us feel ashamed but to help us see that if we want to feel better, then we have to start to make some changes, which are gradual at first. Changing old habits and ways of thinking will with time and work make our personal world a better place to live. Just as the Third Step states that we made a decision to turn our wills and our lives over to the care of God, as we understood God, we believe that our recovery is about decisions and choices. We have to decide a hundred times daily that we are going to turn our lives and our wills over to the care of the God of our understanding. In time we will feel secure enough to put our depression behind us. In other words, our depression will no longer serve a purpose in our life.

We have to acknowledge humbly that I am the one who is having the harsh and negative thoughts about myself, and that I alone must take responsibility for the feelings that I have about myself. I can't continue to blame others for my depression and still think that I will feel better. Dorothy Rowe says that instead of blaming someone else or making someone else the scapegoat of our problems, we need to put aside blame and guilt and think in terms of responsibilities and connections. What she means here is that when she has dealt with depressed people, they seem as though they are carrying the weight of the world and feel responsible for everyone and everything except themselves. She says that when it comes to themselves, they see themselves as totally powerless. We need to look at what is happening in the here and now and take responsibility for our lives, without living in fear of tomorrow and the hurts of yesterday. Humbly ask God to help you live in the now, even if that means living with the temporary horrible pain of depression.

People won't change until they have some assurance that when they do change they will be completely happy. The want to have someone promise them that if they decide to change, they will have no more problems and will be happy. Dorothy Rowe says: "This request is based on two assumptions; namely: 1. Anyone who hasn't got my problems has no problems at all (therefore, when my present problems disappear I shall have no problems); 2. Happiness is total certainty (therefore, unless I know exactly what is going to happen, I cannot be happy)."

Change is risky and some folks don't want to live with risk – they want life to be completely predictable. But with predictability, you pay the price of hopelessness. Hope can exist only when there is uncertainty. You never want anything to change. You want life to be completely under your control.

Pride is not only one of the major sins that we all fall prey to at one time or another in our life, but it is our pride that keeps us from humbly admitting anything at all – namely that I might be the reason that I am depressed. But if you really are sincere in wanting to get out of depression, then you have to be ready to let God remove your shortcomings. Sometimes we hear persons who are continually depressed tell how bad they are and that they can't believe anyone could ever love them if they really got to know them. I find that attitude more on the side of pride than humility, because these people are claiming to be special because they are so bad, rather than to be ordinary like everyone else.

In our prison of depression, we at least know what to expect – it's predictable. There is a certain security in knowing you will always feel the same.

Not only will honesty about ourselves help lead us into areas of a meaningful recovery, but it will allow the Higher Power to quicken our spirit as we honestly face one shortcoming after another and gradually root them out of our lives. We have lived so long with this horrible feeling and are so ashamed to tell anyone how bad we have really felt because they would think we were crazy, that we kept this shameful secret to ourselves. It is only in the telling of the truth of ourselves in a humble and courageous fashion that we will be led to new and healing discoveries within. The more active we become in our own recovery and the more that we live for ourselves, the more we are able to throw off our past inertia and begin to go to meetings and share our lives with others. We will slowly gain a new confidence in ourselves and find out that God does want us with others who are depressed and desires to let His power work in our lives. Just as we have been wounded by our family, our church and our society, so we can be healed by the group - namely the *Depressed Anonymous* group, our new family. It is here that you will find acceptance, nurture and the ability to learn new skills in relating to others. Everyone who is active in the group has already made the decision to turn their lives over to the care of God, as they understand God, and they have admitted that their depression has put their lives out of control. The only thing they have to lose by being a member of *Depressed Anonymous* is their depression.

One member of *Alcoholics Anonymous* said: "The more meetings you attend, the more people you meet at these meetings, the clearer the steps become. We must learn to walk before we can run." In all changes that have to do with our personality, we learn that the change is slow and often painful. In the "letting go" and the surrender that this demands, we have to let God do the work in us. This is the part where we must wait on God and let God continue to do what is best for us. This is when we humbly let go of our choosing to hang on to depression for something we don't know anything about. We worriedly ask: "What will happen to me? Will I survive?"

We have to let God do the work. Let God be in control. Let God do it God's way and in God's time. This is difficult for those who are depressed and who would rather stay in their misery than have a challenge to their addiction to isolation. The Seventh Step prayer mentions how our defects of character stand in the way of being useful to God and our neighbors. God wants to clear away the debris of those hurts and feelings that continue to keep us "holed up" in a bubble of self-seeking, self-pity and fear. The fear is what gets us as we gradually attempt to emerge into the world of unknown avenues. The old tapes in our heads keep playing the same old tune: "You can't be happy!"

In *Depressed Anonymous,* we find honest people talking in honest fashion about how the Higher Power is removing their defects of character and how they are beginning to see some of their feelings to start to lighten up. The acceptance that they find among the members of the group is what helps them relearn the skills necessary to function in their relationships outside the group. The days and hours spent in *Depressed Anonymous* can help us connect with the world again. Healing is about being connected. Our connectedness is being restored, and maybe we never felt connected to a loving God, but instead had felt that our God, as we understood God, was an unmerciful taskmaster who would take away heaven and our loved ones if we were bad. *Depressed Anonymous* and the Twelve Steps help us believe that all you have to do is make a decision to turn our lives over to God. The Higher Power then can prevent our getting lost along the dead-end of blame and self-pity. The Higher Power will get you focused on the blocks that you have set up to defeat yourself. God will let the light in to expose all those areas of your life that have helped you fear the risk of being you and living life to the fullest.

Draw near to God, and God will draw near to you. I believe that this Higher Power, God will definitely lead you to the happiness that you seek. The closer and more often you turn your mind and heart over to this Higher Power, work the program and come to meetings; you will gradually feel and see a new change in your life. It will come as long as you present yourself on a regular basis before the Higher Power with your needs. Remember that to find our way out of depression; you must first admit that you can't get out of depression just by will power alone. We know that we can't just snap out of depression because our whole person, our whole body is involved in this physical numbing of feelings and so we feel disconnected from everything around us. The reason why we have been depressed for so long is not as important as the fact that we admit that we are depressed. Some of the people who come to *Depressed Anonymous* have become depressed only recently due to the loss of a love, loss of self-esteem, and loss of a job or family problems. Usually, depression results from a loss and some swallowed anger about a painful situation in one's life. *Depressed Anonymous* is also very helpful to persons who feel that they have been depressed all their lives, and for the first time are able to put a name on what they have been feeling all these years. Many times, a person's depression stems from a childhood loss, such as a parent dying or leaving because of divorce. This has an effect on a child which may continue into adulthood. As has been mentioned elsewhere, losses of significant people early in life continue to live inside us as we grow older in adulthood. Sometimes these manifest themselves as addictive relationships to other people, and the fear of being abandoned in this type of dependent relationship can cause one to be depressed.

We believe that honesty, openness and a willingness to quit depressing are the basic building blocks of our recovery. To admit our powerlessness and believe that there is a power greater than ourselves is what is going to give my life purpose and hope. And finally we believe that humility is the rock on which each of the Twelve Steps of *Depressed Anonymous* is based. We can say the prayer: "My Creator, I am now willing that you should have all of me – good and bad. I pray that You now remove from me every single defect of character which stands in the way of my usefulness to You and my fellows. Grant me the strength as I go out from here to do your bidding."

Step Eight

Made a list of all persons we had harmed, and became willing to make amends to them all.

One of the dead-end streets that addicted people travel down – often at breakneck speeds – is to blame everyone else for their problems. This indicates an unhealthy mental attitude. In this Step Eight the founders of *Alcoholics Anonymous* saw that if we are to get sober and remain that way then we must look around and take stock of people we have harmed. I mean we must take out the paper and pencil and make a list of all those persons whose lives have been made more difficult because of our depression. We might ask how our depression could possibly hurt anyone. To be living with a person depressed is to experience their lows and feel as trapped as they do. If you have been sad and depressed over any length of time just know that it has adversely affected people around you.

Our depression is such that it has kept us at arm's length and disconnected from other people, friends and family. The first people on our list that we need to make amends to are those who for whatever reason need our word of forgiveness. This Step and the next two (Steps Nine and Ten) have to do with our relationships and the extent to which our depression has damaged our connections between friends and family.

We might want to forgive ourselves for the lack of trust we place in ourselves. After having attended a few more *Depressed Anonymous* meetings, we begin to see ourselves in many of the people who share their stories with the group. We start to get connected with the lives of those around us and begin to look inside ourselves, possibly for the first time, and begin to admit to ourselves how we have cut ourselves off from others. We also need to make amends to those whom we have hurt, ignored or in some way separated ourselves from by our depression.

We at this point need to look at the people whom we have hurt by our sadness and general lack of caring. We need to examine the times when instead of being part of the world around us, we decided to withdraw and isolate ourselves in our own little world. We thrive on telling ourselves how bad we are, how imperfect we are and how no one could genuinely care for us. We wallowed in this self-pity and some of us have even tried to take our own lives. We had convinced ourselves that we were worthless and that there was nothing that we could ever do to change our situation.

I thought that my sadness, fear and social isolation affected only me and so I never thought that my depression, irritability and negativity had any direct effect on those around me. I never realized the extent to which my attitudes and compulsive behavior to sadden myself affected others besides myself. But like all other compulsive behavior and addictions, it is apparent that our lives affect the lives of others.

Once we begin to recover from this addiction and the false security that this provides we learn that by making a list of those persons whom we have harmed we are now willing to make direct amends to them. But you might ask: "Isn't this a little embarrassing?" Yes, it just might be, but it also will bring you a closer step to staying serene and help you continue your program of getting beyond a life lived in continual misery and self-pity.

Feeling worthless, hopeless and helpless we somehow blame everyone else for our sadness. We clutch on to our stubborn denial that our life will never get better or that we can do anything about our own recovery. We need to talk with those people we have harmed by our sadness and show them that we are attempting to change and choose happiness instead of sadness. We tell them that we want to be different and that we are choosing a life filled with hope instead of a life filled with despair.

The list that we make can include family, co-workers, neighbors and others whom we have touched in any negative fashion. We need to get in touch with how our depression has negatively affected our family and how we have used our addiction to sadness to keep us from getting in touch with the feelings and emotions that we have kept bottled up over the years.

It seems to me that the more we share our story with other members of the *Depressed Anonymous* group, the more we can hear for the first time our own unique story. It is amazing how, when we speak to others about ourselves and our addictions, we begin to loosen up and release in ourselves a new sense of ourselves – a freedom to express our true selves. It is at these times when we discuss our addiction at the *Depressed Anonymous* meetings that we get first-hand information and feedback on how others are walking free of their sadness and hollowness.

If our identity is based primarily on our sad mood and sense of futility, then we need to share this feeling with those we make amends to.

Our sadness doesn't exist in isolation. Many times we hear ourselves say that we are "depressives." I personally find this limiting as we are more than just depressed. We never want to assume the identity of being a "depressive" – you might think, act and believe that this is what you will be for the rest of your life. And if we are going to treat depression like any other addiction such as alcoholism, gambling, sexual and love addictions, or overeating, then why not call ourselves what we are, namely: saddicts. If the alcoholic can recover, so can the saddict. I believe the word saddict says it better that the word "depressive". The word saddict promotes the belief that yes, we are addicted to sadness but through the help of the Higher Power, the *Depressed Anonymous* group and the Twelve Steps I can find a way out of my obsession with sadness. The word "depressive" tends not to promote or provide a sense of hope.

Both alcoholic and saddict will recover and find that sought after serenity - as long as they continue to keep honest about their addiction and are alert as to how it keeps them from facing the reality of their lives. We know that our health can be compromised by continued negative emotions and feelings about ourselves. Any intense emotion, such as a continual rumination over out personal worthlessness, for example, can over time cause serious physiological damage. Many people say that the doctor has told them that they have a chemical imbalance and this is what causes their depression. It doesn't cause it – it continues it. The repetitive negative thoughts about oneself, about one's past and/or future are what cause the physiological changes in the brain chemistry and yes, we then have a chemical reaction. The doctor prescribes the tablets that may reduce brain chemistry deficits and one may start feeling better. Some doctors, after prescribing the medication might want to refer you to a counselor so that you may begin to work out the problems that caused the depression in the first place. When you and I begin to work on our life's journey and start to make this list of people we have resentments against, and begin to forgive them, then this is the beginning of making things right in our life. In fact, you might now be feeling better for the first time in your life as you continue to make a conscious effort to take responsibility for your sadness. You realize that you no longer want to stay depressed, but instead are willing to risk feeling better (differently). This is taking the risk of being willing to change. When a person stops smoking, there is a residue craving for nicotine, and the craving is most painful for the first weeks after quitting the addiction. Gradually over time, and due to being able to say no to the impulse to smoke, you feel stronger and so the painful withdrawal becomes less intense. The same applies to the addiction of depression in that at first, it's difficult to stop completely the compulsive repeating of sad thoughts, but with time and working our Twelve Steps and our active involvement in *Depressed Anonymous*, we have the strength to say no to these sad thoughts and begin to choose hope and serenity instead.

In my field of counseling, I always tried to get the family of the depressed person into counseling too so that I might help the person see how their depressing themselves was affecting everyone in the family, including the children. The spouse, if the depressed person was married, always seemed relieved that someone finally could see their viewpoint and understand how they felt and the pain that they too were experiencing. Many times, they would tell how their spouse would never do anything and always put things off until they felt better. But they never feel better! I found much anger and frustration in these relationships, as the spouse was beside himself or herself concerning what to do for their sad partner. They were not only becoming depressed themselves, but they were also feeling guilty about the anger they felt when around the depressed person. How, they thought, could they feel all this anger at someone who was supposed to be sick?

Again we must turn to ourselves and begin to examine our own resentments and grudges, which time after time cause us to sink into a stupor of mournful sadness. Many times our resentments are over how badly we were treated as children and how no one really cared how we felt. These resentments become like lead as they keep our steps heavy and burdensome. We can write down all the people who in any way we have hurt by our depression and resentments. We know by painful experience that the depressed person puts a lot of stock in the past and has a tendency to live there. It is precisely here that we need to jog our memories and ask forgiveness of those persons we feel we have hurt.

You might have on your list one of the multitude of organized religions which you blame for all the bad things that have happened to you in the past and which you keep turning over in your mind. You might want to put on the list a former girlfriend/boyfriend or spouse whom you claim took away all your joy from life, and so you punished them by your continued negativism and angry feelings. When she/he left, you lost all reason for living and resent the fact that he/she married someone else. You might want to put your parents, step-parents, brothers and/or sisters on the list as people whom you need to forgive. You might include in this group some minister, priest, or rabbi whom you have blamed for your problems. You might also want to ask forgiveness of a child or your children for not getting involved and participating more fully in their lives, because you were stewing in your own feelings of worthlessness and guilt. You discover now how that has prevented you from loving others, especially those in your own family who needed it most from you. You have felt shame for not being what you felt you should have been in life and for not living up to the expectations of family, friends and employers. You also need to look at how you need to forgive yourself for not being perfect. You might again want to make amends to your parents who demanded something of you that you could never be. We don't blame here – we forgive.

Maybe I need to make amends to my children for making a clean house the number one priority and never allowing them to give expression to their feelings. Or maybe I was the good daughter or son who never told anyone how I really felt because I was afraid of how my parent(s) would react. Now we might be dredging up all the old feelings of anger and resentment that we have submerged under a mask of kindness and sweetness over the years. We need to voice our anger for having to act like someone that we aren't. I can think of many women who in therapy begin to get in touch with the times when as little girls, they were conditioned to think that good little girls didn't get angry, and so they stuffed and sat upon all these powerful and unpleasant emotions. Feelings that are not expressed can accumulate in our bodies and can't get out until we share them and express them. These stuffed feelings get lodged in our bodies and immobilize us until we feel completely wrung out!

Some have heard all their lives that you shouldn't get angry as mother won't love you anymore. This makes it quite difficult suddenly to shout out our rage and anger at a world that has made women in general feel less than second-class citizens.

In our depression support groups you can come and begin to let out some of those feelings accumulated over the years which have taken their toll on our lives by making us feel helpless and alone. Many women in our culture seemed to have imbibed a helpless feeling with their mother's milk. As women become aware of their abilities and rights as human beings, they begin to experience the freedom that comes from being themselves and throwing aside rules and roles fashioned by men and male minds. Recovery is being able to trust ourselves in exploring ways to feel our emotions.

In most cultures, when males began to depress themselves, they "numb out" and stuff their feelings of hurt, shame, or anger. Males are conditioned to not express in any intimate fashion these unpleasant feelings. One of the positive aspects of our support group is that men can come to our fellowship, share their tears, and know that this is acceptable behavior for any member of the group. What most males really want to do but don't know how is to be intimate with others, sharing those deep feelings. From just an anecdotal account, normally at most *Depressed Anonymous* meetings there are as many men in attendance as there are women, even though the statistics tell us that women are more depressed than men. I too believe that accounting is based on cultural conditioning as well. Women have learned how to talk about feelings more than have men. Women operate on a more relational (intimate) level than do most men. *Depressed Anonymous* is an excellent group for men to not only learn new skills in intimacy, but helps them outgrow old patterns of negative thinking and behavior.

We can at this time add to the list of people we have harmed and be willing to admit to them how we didn't trust them when they said we were good or said we have this or that ability. One of the hardest things for us to accept is that we might have something good going for us. We feel that people can only love us for what we own or how clean our house is or how much money I make at my job. I believed no one could love me for just me. We really never fully trusted anyone, and that included God, our religious leaders, our spouses, our children, and our best friends.

This Step and the next one are the ones that continue our stepping out fearlessly into that brand new world where we daily risk to live with increased hope.

Step Nine

Made direct amends to such people wherever possible, except when to do so would injure them or others.

This step is all about self-appraisal. We need to take this inventory and ask forgiveness of the wrongs that we have done to family, friends and others. We are willing to go to any length to win in this battle over depression and feeling down. We need to forgive others and we need to ask forgiveness of those whom we might have injured by our words and actions. *Alcoholics Anonymous* points out: "This is not an end to itself. Our real purpose is to fit ourselves to be of maximum service to God and the people about us."

We need to look at our relationships now and in the past and see from whom we need to ask forgiveness from for our past wrong actions. There is something therapeutic about seeking forgiveness and being forgiven for past wrongs. It is a fact that once we clear the air of past wrongs, there is released in us a lightness of spirit that can only be experienced by letting go of an old hurt, guilt feeling, or sense of shame. Many persons think that asking for forgiveness would be too embarrassing. Yes, it might be embarrassing, but it will also be a new beginning for you as you give an old resentment or grudge the boot. Just as in the past, our resentments against another gave us the necessary ammunition that we felt we needed to stay in our depression, so here too.

We need first of all at this point to continue with the list of people whom we had hurt. This list must be prayed over and reflected upon so that we can do the proper spring cleaning and have the peace and the serenity promised to those who choose to take responsibility for their own actions. Reaching out to those that we might have harmed by making amends is the only way to continue on the path of recovery. The shame that finally leaves us will free us for the full and firm conviction that I have a right to be on this earth, and yes, I know that even though I am not perfect, I still can be who I want to be, and that's fine.

Fight or flight might be our dilemma as we begin to put some teeth into our recovery program. We might want to flee from those persons we have harmed instead of facing them and making amends to them. This fight or flight emotion applies with equal force to those memories of childhood that might be too painful for us to face, and so we flee them. We find it difficult to get in touch with them. We also might be tempted to fight for our personal pride at times, falsely thinking that we really don't need to make amends to anyone and that we are just fine the way we are.

It is true that we won't ever have a peace and serenity until we make peace with those around us. We want to take a close look at those people who make us feel so small and worthless when we are around them or think of them from our past. We also need to make amends to those persons who made us feel that we were small and worthless, or who made us feel shame about ourselves.

As you continue in your recovery process using these Twelve Steps, you might already find people from the past coming to your mental screen. "Well," you say, "I have been good and I have tried to be perfect, so why am I still so miserable and unhappy?" The reason that you are so unhappy is because you are trying to be perfect, but you never know when you reach perfection as you always have one more line to cross before you become the perfect person that you are struggling so hard to become. Depression is so often a refuge from having to live out our life. And it is only when we feel that we can live with a fair degree of unpredictableness in our lives that we move out of our isolation into the real world. So often our depression hides behind a mask of superficial friendliness – with people never aware of the deep pain that we feel inside. The risk is in moving out of isolation into contact with other depressed people. We know now that it is the expression of our feelings that gets us free. It is the telling and the admission of our powerlessness over our depression that makes us move ever so slowly out of the deep pit of darkness and sadness. So often when we are able to make amends, we feel that part of the prison wall begins to crumble and we begin to see the light of day. We discover a way out! We find that our forgiveness of others frees us and brings us one more step into the peace of serenity. Getting free is in saying that we alone are responsible for our compulsive retreat from life when we run up against some stressful situation. And the more we study and hear about the addictive personalities and behavior, the more we learn about ourselves and how we have anaesthetized ourselves against any possible feeling of pain, hurt, or anger by saddening ourselves and keeping to ourselves.

So often we perceive other people as being stronger than we are. We see people more cheerful and happy than we are, and so we are sure that they cannot really be all that happy when I am feeling so miserable. I need now to make amends to myself for my fear that I might never smile or laugh again. This is the beginning of the end of our saddening – to admit our reluctance to choose life instead of those familiar feelings of sadness.

I know that a number of people who are first introduced to the Twelve Step program wonder what their sadness has to do with this spiritual program of Twelve Steps that originated for alcoholics. I might be depressed, but I am surely not a drunk. Sometimes you will hear a new member of the group say that they never committed any wrong against anyone, so why do they need to make amends? For many persons, the loss of a love, the death of a spouse, the end of a lifetime career can produce a spiraling sense of despair in people whose whole lives have centered on someone or something outside themselves. Many times, these very same people might be co-dependent on others. That is, they are more concerned about someone else's feelings than their own. Their lives are lived for someone else rather than being lived for their own self. When that other person is lost, they feel lost and abandoned. This is precisely the point – the need to make amends for erroneously thinking that someone else can satisfy all their wants and desires. In making amends, we begin to take responsibility for our thoughts and feelings, and when these have hurt others, we need to do something about them.

The depression is so bad at times that we feel no one would ever understand how we feel unless of course they have been there. We just have about given up on God, church, family and friends as allies on our behalf. We feel resentments and anger toward people for not feeling more sympathetic toward our never-ending sadness. We feel that people aren't kind and don't treat us with the same respect that they do other people such as a diabetic, insomniac or arthritic person. Most people don't want anything to do with us because they get tired of our moaning, groaning and pessimistic way of looking at life. Why shouldn't they? Life is tough enough without having to be subjected to another's gloom and doom. But this is the place where we recognize the difference between ourselves and others, and of course we think our lot is always the worst of all. This self-pity never brings us into any personal sense of peace, but has just the opposite effect in that it helps perpetuate the myth that depression floats in like a dark cloud over which we have no control. We need to tell our spouse, family and friends that we want to start again and begin to take charge of our lives and start to chip away at our sadness. We won't blame our need to sadden ourselves on what my wife/husband did or did not do for us, or what a friend said or didn't say. We finally have to take the bull by the horns much like the recovering alcoholic, overeater, gambler or smoker, and admit that it is "I" that has the problem and that it no longer does any good to blame others for my problem. Once I admit that I am addicted to depressing myself, then I can begin to walk through the door of the prison that binds me. I must realize the fact that my depression will only get worse unless I put a stop to all the ill-thinking, feeling and acting out behavior that keeps me perpetually locked into my sadness.

Many times the people we would like to make amends to are dead and long gone – except that they live in our memories. What we can do here is tell our friends about our need to make amends to them and to acknowledge that we have done the best thing that we can do, judging by the circumstances. Many times, our lives have been traumatized from the very beginning of childhood when one or the other parent abandoned us, and we felt that loss deeply so that the sadness of a childhood never lived continues to motivate our every action. Our inability to live with any amount of trust makes it difficult to trust a Higher Power that It too won't abandon us or punish us like an early caretaker did when we were children.

Institutions have many times incurred our wrath and we fear them because they are all powerful and can hurt is if we are not careful, so we watch our thoughts and actions. In fact, we have to be very sure that we are always walking the line with religious institutions because they seem to have a direct line from God. This in itself makes us even more aware of our weakness, vulnerability and shame – just as when we were children. We hate to admit it, but we have had angry and hateful thoughts against these representatives of God who go about so smug and haughty, casting into hell those not on God's special guest list destined for heaven. These feelings that we never share with others are not able to be brought into the open where they are given the light of day.

We also want to caution about rushing headlong into some sort of compulsive need to seek out all those people we need to make amends to. If we go too fast, we might just make ourselves more depressed, as we find that not everyone is as interested in hearing you make amends as you are. As you continue to get in touch with your feelings, stuffed and frozen over the years, you will find that some people might not trust your good intentions and suspect your recent conversion. Some would rather hold off their personal judgments as to whether or not you really want to change and have a more hopeful attitude to life. Don't be too disappointed then if some people aren't as thrilled as you are about your newfound attitudes. The amends that you make to others are for your own recovery – not for someone else.

One of the better ways to make amends is to commit yourself on a daily basis to helping other members of the *Depressed Anonymous* group to find peace and serenity. It is when we each begin to take responsibility and control over our lives and quit blaming the weather, other people, ourselves, institutions, or our jobs for our sadness that we begin to feel more whole in recovery.

Our real purpose is to fit ourselves to be of maximum service to God and the people about us. Yes, there is a long period of reconstruction ahead. We must take the lead. A remorseful mumbling that we are sorry won't fill the bill at all. We ought to sit down with the family and frankly analyze the past as we now see it, being very careful not to criticize them. Their defects may be glaring, but the chances are that our own actions are partly responsible. So we clean house with the family, asking each morning that our Creator show us the way of patience, tolerance, kindness, and love.

Many times each day we pray that the Higher Power manifest itself in us and our lives. We become more like a plate glass window where the light of God's grace continues to shine through us in our lives. The Higher Power is going to make a new path for us to walk as long as we remain in conscious contact with its love, wisdom and guidance.

Step Ten

Continued to take a personal inventory, and when we were wrong, promptly admitted it.

As we continue to keep ourselves free of the thoughts that imprison us ever more tightly with our depression, we begin to recognize that this Power greater than ourselves can and will restore us to sanity. What this breaks down to is that we learn to surrender to this Higher Power as it helps us remove our character defects, enlarges our circle of friendships by our active participation in the *Depressed Anonymous* group, and helps us take a daily inventory of the times when we needed to make amends to others or to ourselves.

Webster's New World Dictionary says that the word "inventory" means "an itemized list or catalogue of goods, property, etc., especially such a list of the stock of business taken annually." We continue to take inventory during our day and see whether we have not dealt honestly with past hurts, angry feelings, guilt, bitterness, fear, shame, boredom, stress, poor diet, too little or too much sleep, pessimism, rigidity, dwelling in the past, worrying about the future, feeling insecure and not trusting, feeling misunderstood, and finally the possible use of drugs, including the drug of alcohol. We look at this list and work on a particular character defect and use it as a discussion lead for one of our Twelve Step depression group meetings. This is an inventory and it is not taken to make us feel sad but to help us see that it is only in naming the enemy that we can free ourselves from what has held us captive in the past. This is what has built our wall of depression in the past. Call these character defects the bricks that have been used to imprison ourselves in our isolation and confining lifestyle.

For us who have experienced depression over a long time, we need to examine whether our sadness comes from "feeling sorry" for ourselves or for some other reason. Sometimes we need to ask ourselves: "Is self-pity getting in the way of my recovery?" If we think that it is, then we need to look at the basic cause of our "feeling sorry" for ourselves. Many times we find that resentment over a past injustice to ourselves is the culprit. Or maybe it is something that we have done in the past that we feel we can't or haven't forgiven ourselves for. Sometimes we feel that we haven't been treated fairly, and that makes us continue to feel sad. Also, as we have mentioned frequently before in this work, our sadness may go back to our childhood resulting from a traumatic situation such as a parent dying, divorcing or abandoning us. Many times, just being willing to face this will enable us to process the mourning of a lost childhood, a lost parent or a lost self-identity as a person. We need to do the grief work and mourn this loss in our early life. And so grieving a loss goes through a number of predictable stages and these stages must be experienced if one is to experience a life free of the sadness that might have been hurting for many years.

Many times, persons depressed find that the more they get in touch with their feelings, painful as that might be, the more they need to remain with the feelings and really feel them. This is the beginning of getting free from their tyranny. We have to get in touch with our feelings of anger, sadness, and the fact of our denial that we have experienced the fierce feelings of rejection so early in life. There may be some covered over rage resulting from this unpleasant childhood experience. It's amazing to hear people say that as children, they never had a birthday party. We also know that sadness, guilt, shame and a few other losses coming at one time in our life can slowly push us over the line as we find ourselves overwhelmed with stress and feelings of defeat. It's this subtle feeling of being out of control that brings deepening sadness until we finally become immobilized.

Many times just writing down what you are feeling will help you get rid of the pain of that particular feeling. Also, when you speak to someone about how you are experiencing an unpleasant feeling, then others can and will be there with you through the pain. Many persons who are in recovery keep a feelings journal in which they list the various feelings that they experience from one time to another during their day. It's wise to try to stay with these unpleasant feelings and sort out where they are coming from and how we caused them. Many times when we describe what we feel, we begin to release in ourselves the "stuckness" that keeps us in a mood of hopelessness.

Denial and rationalization, both forms of defense against getting in touch with our compulsion to sadden ourselves, need to be eliminated if we are to live life with hope and start to relish the unpredictability of it all. If you really are working on the program, you will begin to see that your recovery is your choice. I can't make you happy. You have to choose to be happy.

Many times we who depress ourselves find that we have placed a wide gulf between what we are and what we would like to be. We have such high standards that we can never reach them, so that we fall back into despair time after time, which gives credence to the fact that we really are bad and worthless. We always want to be the controller. I like what Dorothy Rowe says: "The desire for perfect control, of the environment and of oneself, is based on a profound mistrust of the controller. Because you see yourself as bad, you cannot trust yourself to be. Because you cannot trust yourself to become, to allow yourself to grow as a plant grows."

Many times the fear of letting go is a problem for the compulsive person addicted to his/her sadness. One of the many beneficial aspects of living out the Twelve Step program is that we can take a daily inventory of our lives, and we promptly need to admit when we are wrong. This takes some courage because once you believe that you are perfect, it's difficult to admit that you need to make amends.

We come to believe that if we do consider ourselves bad and worthless, we just know that no one can really love us or accept us. We just know the more we look at ourselves and our few remaining relationships, that we really aren't accepted – people just put up with us. "…There is one great advantage about seeing yourself as helpless and in the power of others. You don't have to be responsible for yourself. Other people make all the decisions and when things turn out badly you can blame other people. And things always turn out badly. You know this. That's why you always expect the worst."

Responsibility is the name of the game in recovery and it is here that we need to focus our attention. As we get into a discussion with other people who are depressed, much like ourselves, we see that they talk about feeling better while at the same time acting on their own behalf. These people who are doing better are also talking about taking charge of their lives and doing things for themselves instead of constantly trying to please others. In fact, at *Depressed Anonymous* meetings, the recovering people often delight at how assertive they are becoming now that they have gained a sense of mastery over their lives. They are also committed to their own recovery. People who want to change begin to swallow their pride and ask for help. They begin to get in touch with their feelings and feel! This is truth and this is getting in touch with one's best self.

"As you well know, when we say we are wrong, we create an area of uncertainty…if you cannot tolerate uncertainty, then you cannot afford to admit that you are wrong. Absolute certainty may appear to you to be a wonderful thing, giving complete security, but have you ever considered that if you want absolute certainty, you must give up freedom, love and hope."

This seems to be the main fear for us when depressed, namely, that we won't have our world in our complete control. I think this is where we need to talk to members of our group or we need promptly to admit that we were wrong. The group is the best forum of peers where we can express our deepest fears about losing control and not try to force the world to be as we feel it should be.

Resentments also have a powerful way of getting us sad as we remember all the hurts that have been part of our days and our lives. We can stay in our addiction and build a museum filled with skeletons of our past hurts, or we can face them, deal with them and move on in the process of our recovery. We need to deal face to face with all our old hurts and then name them and remove them from our lives once and for all. We need to hand them over to the Higher Power and let its desire move them where it will.

We need to get in touch with those feelings from our early childhood days and try to remember when we made ourselves sad and what situation today makes us feel sad. There sometimes is a connection between the two. We know this return to early childhood feelings is one of the best ways to get a beginning in our self-healing. We can talk about how we felt about our mother and father, and how our relationship with them was lived out in childhood. Can we connect with any early childhood event that upon reflection makes us feel sad? Usually, this childhood event with its feeling of shame, sadness or guilt is reactivated whenever we come upon a similar incident in our present adult life. Is there some fear of authority figures in our present life? Do we fear other people's anger? What makes us cringe when we feel our feelings will be hurt? These questions about our early childhood and these unpleasant early life experiences still live in our flesh today. It is good when we get in touch with our sadness today, find out what triggers it and then try to go back and see whether the present sadness reminds us of something we felt sad about a long time ago. This is one other road that can lead us out of our sadness.

A member of our group said that her father was very authoritarian and strict. She said that she was always trying to please him and do the best she could with everything he wanted. She said that she could never do things well enough to please him. Even today, she still tries to please others, but because of her perfectionist nature finds herself always inadequate and never satisfied with herself. This produces a feeling of loss as she feels guilty over losing control over those situations in which she wants to excel.

She also feels resentments towards other people as they never seem to notice all her outstanding qualities.

Sometimes persons tell us that they get sad for no reason at all. All of a sudden, they just feel down and don't know why. Many times after reflecting upon this sudden rush of sadness, they realize that it has come from somewhere and they might as well take responsibility for it and deal with it. One of the best ways to deal with a feeling, especially the unpleasant ones, is to stay with it, feel it, and see what it is trying to say to you. When we run from it we lose. Granted, this won't be easy and you might not find the source of the sudden sadness at the first glance, but in time you can feel it, deal with it and then discard it. The more you ruminate about how sad you are and then how bad you are for being so sad, the more you have begun the downward spiral into physically feeling weak and hopeless. This is the time to call a friend or a member of the group. Just say: "Hey, I'm feeling sad and here is the reason why I think I am feeling sad – what do you think?" More times than not, your sad feelings will melt away.

But you want absolute certainty and you have too much pride to admit that you could be wrong. You take pride in seeing yourself as essentially bad; in not loving and accepting other people; in the starkness and harshness of your philosophy of life. You take pride in the sorrows of your past and the blackness of your future; pride in recognizing the evil of anger; pride in not forgiving; pride in your humility; pride in your high standards; pride in your sensitivity; pride in your refusal to lose face by being rejected; pride in your pessimism; pride in your martyrdom; pride in your suffering.

The basic premise about ourselves that has to be faced is that if we truly do see ourselves as bad and worthless, then we have to get up off our backs and begin to forgive ourselves and humbly share that we no longer want the misery of our depression. We want to take a risk and face our pride, and work at changing ourselves. Dorothy Rowe's list of prides really takes the steam out of anyone wanting to feel sorry for themselves.

The real risk is when that first inkling comes that because of your active and regular work in the Twelve Step depression group, you begin to feel a small bit of serenity growing inside you. This is what scares us all. Our guilt, our shame, our losses in life have almost completely shut down our sense of spontaneity and playfulness so that we are afraid of the new way we are feeling. Our first thought is that it won't and can't last. That is when we need to face the fear, stay with it, and it will flee. As long as you stay with these unpleasant feelings, keep working on yourself at meetings and just tell yourself that you can beat these negative attitudes about yourself, your future and your world, you can start to rebuild.

At this time, call a friend and tell them you need help rebuilding. Instead of allowing your defects of character to imprison you, you are now using those bricks to build a bridge between you and those other members of the group who want to free themselves from the isolating feelings of sadness and hurt.

"Promptly" means at once, and this is especially good for all of us, because when we are depressing, we like to go off and ruminate and sadden ourselves as to how guilty and bad we are. We need to turn this around so that instead of beating ourselves over the head, we need "promptly" to admit that we are saddening ourselves and so free ourselves from the cycle of sad thoughts and begin to distract ourselves by engaging in some positive and pleasurable activity on your own behalf. "Promptly" also means to express a feeling as soon as you feel it. In the past, we had the tendency to keep it locked up in ourselves as it got stuck, frozen and unattended to. So feel safe to express what you are feeling, and take credit for its being your feeling, that it doesn't belong to someone else. People stress that when you feel something, you should say: "I feel mad" or "I feel happy" or "I feel upset." The point here is just saying "I" makes a big difference in how you feel. If you say: "You make me angry" or "You make me sad" or "You make me upset," this only misplaces the source of your feeling. You need to take full responsibility for how you feel – you can't blame it on anybody else.

Promptly forgive ourselves! Promptly tell a friend, a *Depressed Anonymous* group member, co-worker, or spouse that you are now trying to live one day, one hour at a time and are depending on the Higher Power to give you the courage to risk thinking hopeful thoughts which have the power to lead yourself back into the community, the family and among friends. Develop a gratitude attitude and thank God for today! This day is all we have. Get involved in your own healing. Start to take on the attitude that if other people can make it, then so can I. It's true – you can make it if you follow this program.

"Human beings are never quite alike, so each of us, making an inventory, will need to determine what our individual character defects are. Having found the shoes that fit, we ought to step into them and walk with new confidence that we are at last on the right track."

Step Eleven

Sought through prayer and meditation to improve our conscious contact with God, as we understood God, praying only for knowledge of God's will for us and the power to carry it out.

With our compulsion to sadden ourselves, much like the alcoholic's urge to medicate himself or herself with alcohol, we need daily to turn our wills over to God and ask for the Higher Power's guidance. Eventually, it is the conscious contact with this loving God that sets us free from the need to sadden ourselves.

All of us who are substance addicted (compulsive overeating, alcohol, cocaine, prescription medications) or process addicted – addicted to a behavior (the workaholic, sex, gambling, depression) know that in order to free ourselves from the intoxicating experience, we have to first want to give it up and live without it. We best do this one day or one hour at a time. Don't say you will quit a self-destructive behavior for one year and then see how you do. No, try to live one day at a time – it's a lot easier. As someone once said: "If you want to eat an elephant, the best way to do it is one bite at a time." We know from past experience that our sobriety, our disappearance of sadness is due to letting go – admitting my powerlessness over my sadness and turning it over to my Higher Power and letting it take care of my sadness. I can't do anything to remove my compulsive behavior until I choose to live without it.

When we are especially depressed, it's hard to keep our mind on things such as prayer, but with continued effort and practice, we can come to believe that whatever we are doing just might be better than sitting in our own pool of self-pity. If we haven't ever been big on "organized religion," we have a good chance that this new approach to being with God is much less judgmental, and that this God of the Twelve Steps is much more accepting than other concepts of God that we might once have held. Sometimes we have found that our religious background has filled us with a large amount of crippling guilt, shame and hopelessness rather than the complete acceptance that we will receive from our Higher Power.

Praying means to ask for something. We ask that we might let God take over our lives since we have admitted that we are powerless over saddening ourselves and that our lives have become un-manageable. As it says in *Alcoholics Anonymous*: "I saw that it was my LIFE that was un-manageable – not just my drinking." I believe there is much wisdom in that short statement, and it is one that I want to reflect upon. The fact that we have pretty much shut ourselves off from the world is not a very sane thing to do when one of our human species' major characteristics is being a social creature.

Our continual saddening of ourselves pushes us away from any form of pleasant interaction with others and continually builds the wall higher for our depression. This is the purpose of our continually making conscious contact with the God of our understanding. I do believe, and I speak from my own experience that the Higher Power respects our surrender and our letting it take charge of our lives. It is amazing how in our recovery, our feelings start to thaw out. We feel some emotions, and the healing begins. For us who are depressing ourselves, we can learn that the best way to break free from this chronic sadness is just to admit that we are responsible for our sadness and then pray to God that we want to be serene and happy. We just pray to be free, and gradually with small steps and subtle changes taking place inside ourselves, we feel a change occurring.

Every so often, we come into contact with a person, place or circumstance that causes us some uncomfortableness and we start to withdraw into the comfort of our depression. It is here that we have dumped our trust of the Higher Power and choose the comfort of our sadness instead.

After falling back into our old comfortable habit of depressing ourselves, we then realize we have gotten ourselves right back where we started – depressed and feeling isolated. We realize that all we have is today. As *Alcoholics Anonymous* points out: "The poorest person has no less and the wealthiest has no more – each of has but one day. What we do with it is our own business, and how we use it is up to us individually."

I remember Fred on his first visit to *Depressed Anonymous*. He said that he had been depressed all his life. The group listened to Fred, and of course for the most part, Fred said he didn't have the foggiest notion what all this talk of God had to do with his sadness and how it was supposed to help him. But it was the pain of Fred's depression that brought him back time after time to the meetings, and he started not only to feel better, but he began to look better. Then as he heard about the Twelve Steps, he saw that he could trust this Higher Power, and that maybe the depression that had been such a lifetime companion was not for him anymore. Fred took the plunge, came to believe that a Power greater than himself could restore him to sanity – and it did just that. Fred said that he didn't need his depression any more, got busy making amends to family, friends and co-workers for being such a negative person, and began to take inventory where he needed to spring clean his house. In time, Fred began to reach out to others in the group, and he began to understand how he had become like many others in the group – a saddict. Depression for many was an addiction to sadness. The only way out of Fred's addiction was to let go of it, admit his life was un-manageable and start to work on himself and his character defects. Fred still keeps coming back to the meetings to share his story with others on the how of his recovery. He talks about the way it was before *Depressed Anonymous*, and the way it is now since he has been working the steps and handed his life over to the Higher Power.

Yes, Fred is tempted to sadden himself now and again, but with his dependence on the Higher Power, he no longer falls under the compulsion of giving in to the sadness. He is finding that he can choose to be happy, and it is in his daily prayer and meditation times that he feels led by the Higher Power for the day ahead.

Alcoholics Anonymous says that being honest means telling yourself the truth. Also, the *Alcoholics Anonymous* pioneers believed that the Higher Power was at anyone's behest, as long as they at least made an effort to contact It.

"We found God does not make too hard terms with those who seek It's guidance. To us, the Realm of Spirit is broad, roomy, all inclusive, and never exclusive or forbidding to those who earnestly seek it. It is open, we believe, to all men and women."

We believe that to be conscious is to have been able first of all to listen to someone or something that expresses God's desire to free us from our misery as soon as we are willing to turn our minds and our wills over to it. Somewhere along the way, we were convinced that the only safe way to make this life bearable and predictable was to continually sadden ourselves, withdraw into our little shell and make sure that our own small world was completely under our control. It was a perfect little world, this would of ours. It was dark, gloomy and painful, but at least we knew what we had. It is this predictableness that makes life inescapably hell for all of us, even though we'd rather have this than the total surprise of living.

The more we are being led by the Higher Power, the more we will be alert to the signals that something positive is beginning to work for us in our life. As we become more desirous of making conscious contact with the Higher Power, the more peace and serenity start to flow into our lives. We soon experience a peace that we have never experienced before, and we find that we want more of it as we daily make up our mind and get into contact with the Higher Power. This prayer and meditation, or "P&M" as some people in the group call it, makes us ever more aware that it is this spiritual approach that makes our depression less and less of a negative force to be reckoned with in our lives.

Just sitting back and relaxing is a difficult thing to do when we are depressed, but if we want to have the Higher Power work in our lives, then we have to quiet ourselves and listen often to Its promptings. Listen then and pray. Pray that you might free this sadness in yourself as you continue to work the steps of this program. The more you live with a gratitude attitude, the more you will see that life is worth living and that you can live with the unpredictable. Life is supposed to be predictable and the reason why is that each of us lets God's power unfold in our lives. The more conscious and aware we are of its operating in our universe, the more serenity we have in our lives. We believe that as we take a daily inventory and really work at getting in touch with God, then God will reciprocally get in touch with us. It won't be long until our meditation will produce in us a feeling that God is guiding our lives and that Its love is putting us back on our feet. We are finding that we want to risk testing out our wings and so we try to live one day at a time and forget about the hurts, fears and pain of yesterday, or the anxious moments that we might face tomorrow. The members of the group call these the: "What if this happens or what if that happens?" The Higher Power is only today. It's not yesterday or tomorrow. It lives now. It lives in our hearts and all it wants and desires is that we make contact with It, and then Its force will unfold as time continues. With time, It will manifest Itself in our minds and hearts.

We only desire God's will for us. How often in the past was I scared to turn my will over to God and let It do with me as It willed. No way! I wasn't going to have God take over my life and take away all my control. Who knows, God might send me to some God-forsaken island somewhere to talk about God. I wouldn't dare turn over my free will to anything like that. I wanted to stay in control, and the way to do that was by not turning my will over to anyone, especially God. This does say something about our feeling about God doesn't it? Namely that we have received the freedom to make ourselves miserable if we like by not trusting, or we can trust and start to work our way out of the darkness of our depression. It is completely up to us, if we so choose. We pray for the knowledge of God's will and the power to carry it out. This is another big sentence. The way to pray for the knowledge of God's will is continually to make amends to those that we have hurt and promptly to ask forgiveness. There is no room in our recovery for holding on to resentments – this just throws us into sadness and isolation and keeps us in our compulsion to repeat our addictive lifestyles. We continue to feel slights by others as the greatest rejection, and of course this causes us to sadden ourselves even more.

We find that no one need have difficulty with the spirituality of the program. Willingness, honesty and open mindedness are the essentials of recovery. But these are indispensable.

There is a principle which is a bar against all information – which is proof against all arguments and which cannot fail to keep a man in everlasting ignorance – that principle is contempt prior to investigation.

We can see from this then that persons who have at least the desire to stop their compulsive behavior to depress can have a chance by following this Twelve Step recovery program. This God consciousness is what makes the program of *Depressed Anonymous* work and is at its very core.

We wish to say that any alcoholic capable of honestly facing his/her problem in the light of our experience can recover, provided that he/she does not close their mind to all spiritual concepts. He/she can only be defeated by an attitude of intolerance or belligerent denial.

Steps Two and Three, like Step Eleven, are concerned with our wills being in God's will. We should seek, as a priority, knowledge of God's will for us. But the recovery is up to you. You have to be willing to admit that your life is un-manageable - your sadness is out of control. You are honest enough to admit that your pride is blocking you from choosing to get you undepressed.

As it says in *Alcoholics Anonymous*, if someone wants to know how the program works, it is "H" for honesty, "O" for open mindedness, and "W" for willingness.

Depressed Anonymous finds that just a willingness to believe is enough to start a person's program of recovery. The desire to free myself from the pain of my sadness becomes greater than the hold that the sadness of the depression has over me.

We also believe that we saddicts are like men/women who have lost their legs, and they never grow new ones. We have to conclude that since our depression and sad thoughts are getting progressively worse over the course of time, we then have to admit that our feelings are out of control and that we need help.

I very much like the whole spiritual orientation of the Twelve Step way of life – and just because we are a spiritual program doesn't mean that we are denying the importance of other religious organizations or faiths. I feel that the greatest gift I have ever received is to know that I have an addictive compulsion to depress myself – it is this reality that brought me into the fellowship of *Depressed Anonymous*. It is here that I came in contact with and found a nonjudgmental God who cared for me so much that God was willing to wait for me to reach out and receive such love.

The central fact of our lives today is the absolute certainty that our Creator has centered into our hearts and lives in a way which is indeed miraculous. It has commenced to accomplish those things for us which we could never do by ourselves.

There is a complete transformation in our lives that begins to take place when all our old ideas are replaced by new, fresh and life giving ideas. One can become a new person here.

One remembers the prayer of St. Francis where he prays to be a channel of God's grace. This is where we come in. Those of us in the program want to be a force for good in this world, and what greater good can you do for the world than to tell people depressed how being open to the will of God has helped free you of depressed thoughts and feelings? Also by choosing to re-kin ourselves by developing new friendships with others in the *Depressed Anonymous* group, we gradually get in touch with the frightened small child inside us. We can begin to get in touch with childhood hurts and quit looking forever for mother and father figures to approve of us and affirm us. Our addiction to getting other's approval begins to wither as we share our story with our new family, the Twelve Step group. We begin to re-parent our child inside and gradually we work through our feelings of shame and sadness. Remember, we don't want to tell God how to run our life. We just want to pray that God will do with us as God wills.

Meditation is getting still inside and listening to the voice and guidance of God. We are very active in meditation even though we let God speak to us. We are receptive to God's every prompting of wisdom and love. We have no desire but to desire God's will. We are no longer dependant on our will, but God's will is what guides us.

Before the day begins, we first thank God for the privilege of doing God's will today and the time that God has given us. We just ask for the courage to carry out God's will in our lives this day We pray for the serenity that comes from surrendering our will to God's. We need to keep our life simple. We need to take it easy and not get over involved and overwhelmed by countless duties and concerns. The enormity of life will throw us back into depression unless we start to live with more wisdom and circumspection. Each morning during our meditation, we ask that the Creator show us the way of patience, tolerance, kindliness and love.

We think about the twenty-four hours ahead when we wake up, and attempt to live the day in honesty and peace. We ask God to ward off thoughts of self seeking, dishonesty and false motives. As *Alcoholics Anonymous* says, when we are faced with the indecision about something, we then ask God for inspiration and we let go of struggling for an answer. *Alcoholics Anonymous* says that you will be surprised at how the right answers will come after we have practiced this way of living. It also comes to pass that our hunches are more right than wrong. We also pause throughout the day when we are fearful, puzzled or anxious. We pray to the Higher Power for which direction to take. I like this suggestion the best when *Alcoholics Anonymous* says: "We constantly remind ourselves that we are no longer running the show, humbly saying to ourselves many times each day 'Thy will be done.' " We are then in much less danger of excitement, fear, anger, worry, self-pity, or foolish decisions. We become more efficient. We do not tire so easily, for we are not burning up energy foolishly as we did when we were trying to arrange life to suit ourselves. By coming to the meetings and admitting our addictions, we finally get in touch with those emotions that have all but shut down from an early time in our lives, when to feel hurt too much. We now have the chance to let these feelings get displayed and expressed in the supportive and trusting environment of our newly chosen family of the *Depressed Anonymous* group.

Our feelings expressed and positively received by the group allow us then to focus on the way we think about ourselves, and make it possible for us to parent ourselves instead of continually seeking out the lost unavailable parent in the guise of multiple sexual relationships, alcohol, gambling, and any of the many other compulsions that are used to fill the void in our lives.

Practicing the program enables us to be led by the Higher Power to do the most good that we can and which our Higher Power wants us to do.

The beautiful thing about God is that God is simple. There are not parts to God – no body, mind and soul. We see God as a oneness and are only praying for knowledge of God's will and the power to carry it out. That says so much. It says that we don't pray for ourselves unless we are praying that God use us for the growth of someone else. But right now, we want to ask that we have the knowledge of its will. This is where we pray that we might listen quietly for the still small voice that already dwells in each of our hearts (the Kingdom of God lies within) and comes to light the more we make time for it to speak. The more you get attuned to listening, the more you will hear and be led. There is no doubt about it. It takes time and practice. For the depressed person like yourself, you will find that the only voices you heard were the old tapes that kept playing in your head, reminding you how bad and worthless you were. Now you are hearing how, if you trust in the Higher Power, you will begin to feel better.

Talk to God about how you can get out of the pit that you're in – then listen. In time, you can hear the solution to your question. This is a trust relationship with your God.

A recovering alcoholic said: "In the Twelve Steps, the word "God" is mentioned seven times, but the particular addiction – alcohol, drugs, gambling, etc. is only mentioned once, in the First Step. After a while, you become so close to God, you really depend on God not just at prayer time, but all day long."

We want only to know God's will because if your will is lined up with God's will, then everything that you need or want is all there. It's very liberating to desire only that your will be in God's will. The more you pray, the more you will want to be in God's will. Your saddiction will be a thing of the past and the peace of God will be a thing of the now.

We are able to heal the sadness that goes deep into our very soul only by the surrender of ourselves to the Higher Power and by trusting our sadness and despair to the members of the Twelve Step group. You begin to feel completely and unconditionally accepted by this group of people involved with their issues – many times going all the way back to a childhood in which they were unloved and abandoned. Some were not physically abandoned, like a parent leaving home or a parent dying, but they were abandoned in the sense that no one ever loved them and told them how special they were. We know that it is this feeling of being abandoned that sets us up for our addictions as we continue to search out someone or something to make us feel good. This great void in our lives will always leave us saddened until the day that we can name it, admit we need help, and turn our life and our will over to the care of God, as we understand God. This will help us face the shame and heal the not-OKness of ourselves. We will grieve the childhood that never was and begin the work of re-parenting the child within.

Getting free of our saddiction is to learn how to prize ourselves. The God of our understanding will give us the power to carry out its will for our lives. This God, as you understand God, will help you put your life back together and begin to feel other emotions and energy besides the unpleasant ones so familiar to you most of your life. You can try to heal yourself on your own, but that can be very difficult. To be healed and to find acceptance for yourself is accomplished only through the power of the group. It is in the group working the Twelve Steps that you will find your way out of your depression. Try it and live.

We admit that our life is un-manageable and it is only when we are willing to let the Higher Power take control of our lives that we will grow and find the serenity and peace that all heart's desire. Our dependence on the Higher Power helps us become more independent of our need to sadden ourselves.

Step Twelve

Having had a spiritual awakening as the result of these Steps, we tried to carry this message to the depressed, and to practice these principles in all of our affairs.

The only requirement for membership in *Depressed Anonymous* is a sincere desire to quit saddening ourselves today - just for this twenty-four hour period. We want to try for this short period of time to let go of our sadness. But since we are saddicts, we need to know that we can't just snap out of our sadness in minutes or even days. To get to feeling better takes time because our learning to sadden ourselves goes back over months, possibly years and one doesn't just snap out of feeling bad in a few days when this whole way of living has taken years to develop. As was brought out in another Step, it's not so much our addiction that we need to focus on, as our whole life - which we now admit is un-manageable. By practicing the principles of the Twelve Steps, we now know that we need to make an inventory of our whole life. We can leave no rock unturned if we want to live with serenity and hope. Our sadness, like any other addiction, is merely a symptom of some deeper compulsion that manifests itself in our need to seek comfort and safety in sadness. But this is the nature of our addictive behavior and thinking. Our thinking has been compulsive. Every time someone hurts our feelings, and said something that wasn't pleasant, we withdrew into the dark hole of our depression. We shut down our feelings by numbing ourselves against future hurts. *Depressed Anonymous* wants you and me to try for one day at a time not to withdraw compulsively into sadness when we come up against a stressful situation.

We now know that it is only when we actively involve ourselves in the first step of *Depressed Anonymous* that we start the march toward recovery and to living a life that can be serene and filled with hope. Hope is what we seek as people depressed. We refuse to label ourselves as depressives because we do not intend to be depressed any longer than we have to. We are also a lot more than our feelings of sadness. Our real identity is emerging from the sadness as we try to live one day at a time.

Even though we have been accustomed to live in the past and see our world as a threat and danger, we find ourselves in a fellowship of men and women who by their own admission recognize that they caused their depression and were afraid to get out of it because to experience any feeling other than sadness would be too unfamiliar and frightening.

The fellowship of *Depressed Anonymous* is made up of members who are working the program, who have had a spiritual awakening and want to share their story of how it is now, now that they have admitted that they are saddicts and how they came to believe that a power greater than themselves could restore them to sanity. This sharing from older members only gives a sense of courage to the newcomer. We know we only have today to live our life and we want to live with hope today because today is all we have. Yesterday is gone forever and tomorrow isn't here yet.

These Twelve Steps work for those who work the program and who try to live one day at a time. Many times we have been so scared of being rejected once more that we have withdrawn deeper into the anguish of our shame and hurt. We need to air our hurts, our shame, and let others hear our story. There is something healing about hearing ourselves speak to others about our own journey in life and the many emotional potholes that we have fallen into from time to time. We have felt our lives were jinxed! But now we can begin to feel hopeful when other members of the group shake their heads in knowing approval of what we are saying when we tell our story. Most have been where we are now. And the more we make an effort to come to meetings regularly, the more we will find members of the group telling us how they are seeing a change in the way we act, talk, and look. We will accept the group's comments as being true and honestly expressed. These people speak our language and they all have been where we are now. You gradually begin to see yourself as healer instead of victim the more you work this program and get excited about the possibility of helping others. When you start reaching out to others in the group, it is at that point that you are carrying the message of hope to others. You have a future with *Depressed Anonymous.*

We all know that any addiction and compulsive type of behavior gradually removes you from the regular activities of persons around you, including family, friends, and co-workers until you are established in the narrow confines of pain and isolation. We are always going to be just a little more isolated the more we try to think our addiction through in the circle of our own thoughts. Most of us need the fellowship of the group to keep ourselves honest and in recovery and our dark thoughts out in the open.

Having had a spiritual awakening means that we are now aware that the core of our being is spiritual and is where our power resides. "The Kingdom of God is within you." This spiritual awakening occurred when we finally let the God of our understanding enter our lives and we surrendered our resistance to getting better. We soon discover in the programs that no compulsion can be controlled by will power alone. It must be surrendered to the Higher Power or to the care of the God of our understanding. It alone will remove in time the burden from our backs. This is the spiritual awakening that keeps us free from sadness as we take the message of healing to others in the group who are new to the program. We admit that we make no promises to anyone and that there will be no magic answers and quick solutions to their saddiction. No, it all takes time and this is the message of the group. Such slogans as: "Take it easy," "Keep it simple," and "Easy does it" are all meant to help you and me to live one day at a time and continue to try to live with serenity. When we practice these steps on a daily basis, starting our day with asking the Higher Power for guidance for the rest of the day, we can then be assured of God's presence and help in our lives.

When you have walked the program and worked the Steps and turned your life over to the God of your understanding, you will clean house and make amends where needed and let the Higher Power be manifest in your life.

We don't need to call or label someone a saddict. Let them discover that for themselves after they hear our own stories. We want to tell them the way it was before *Depressed Anonymous* and how it is now that we are living the *Depressed Anonymous* Twelve Step program. Once newcomers hear the "before" and "after" of our lives, it will make it easier for them to believe us when they experience our own enthusiasm and cheerfulness. They will believe that our recovery isn't put on. Also, our hopeful witness to our recovery is the best witness that the Twelve Step program works. There are two kinds of saddicts: 1) - the recovering saddict. The one who is working the Twelve Step program and is aware of how his/her addiction to sadness is ruining his/her life; and 2) - the miserable saddict. The one who continues to deny and/or rationalizes that he/she can choose to feel something different from sadness.

"Both you and the new man/woman must walk day by day in the path of spiritual progress. If you persist, remarkable things will happen. When we look back, we realize that the things which came to us when we put ourselves in God's hands were better than anything we could have planned.

Follow the dictates of a Higher Power and you will presently live in a new and wonderful world, no matter what your present circumstances."

What a promise!

Remarkable things happen to us when we are willing to admit defeat and talk about our powerlessness over our depression and how our lives had become un-manageable. This first step is the beginning of the flight of steps that takes us up and into our new way of living. At our fellowship of *Depressed Anonymous* we talk hope, we act hopeful, and we think hope. We learn that our thinking depressed and negative thoughts might have gotten us in the shape that we are in today. What you think is what you become. For us who find sadness our second nature, we at times continue to revert to the comfort of old familiar negative thinking and are in actuality returning to self-destructive activity. Hope is overcome by sadness.

When we became convinced that a Power greater than ourselves could restore us to sanity, we found ourselves turning many times during a twenty-four hour period to that power. It is a rock in a rocky sea that we all hold on to when we find it easier just to give up and sadden ourselves, instead of facing the storm and living through the fear. What Bill W. said about the alcoholic applies equally to the saddict: "He/she can settle for mediocrity and self-satisfaction even though this may indeed prove to be a precarious perch. Or he/she can choose to go on growing in greatness of spirit and action."

You never stop using and following the steps of the program. We are in recovery all our lives. You don't graduate. When we return to saddening ourselves, we return to the old compulsion that can again reduce us to that bankrupt individual who is bereft of peace and hope. We want to grow in the conviction that the Higher Power will restore us to sanity. One of the best ways to grow out of our saddiction is to start acting the healer instead of being the passive victim. We are under the care of no one except our God.

This spiritual awakening is enhanced even further when we make a decision to turn our wills and our minds over to the care of God. Without a doubt this is a very big step for many people to trust anybody – and now especially a God who they have spent a lifetime fearing. It is this decision which allows us to feel freedom when we start to practice the daily turning over of our will to God. It frees us up, and as we pray and listen in our meditation times, we find that our spiritual capacity to connect with the Higher Power is greatly magnified.

Now we have to look at ourselves and do some housecleaning. We have to start listening to others in the group when they talk about Steps Four and Five, because these are the critical steps that free us from the guilt, shame, and burdens of perfectionism and the need for control that we have carried within ourselves all these years. The practice of making this fearless and moral inventory of ourselves on a daily basis, especially at the end of our day, brings us up to date on how we have been living the program. It also helps us take an active role in removing the bricks that make up the walls of our prison of depression.

Practicing these principles keeps us in tune on a daily basis and helps us keep our hope strong enough so that we can move away from our compulsion to sadden ourselves. When we are within the fellowship of *Depressed Anonymous* we learn how we are the ones responsible for our recovery, and that we can't blame our spouses, children, co-workers, or anyone else for our depressed state.

Humility is the response to honesty. The more honest we are, the more we are willing and able to think humbly about ourselves. Over time, our narcissistic attitudes will gradually wither away as we continue to deal honestly with our lives and work the Twelve Step program.

Making a list of everyone we had hurt and being willing to make amends to them all is another road to serenity and happiness. We are willing to clear out all the wreckage of our past lives, with our resentments and hurts being admitted up front. We also need to ask forgiveness from all those whom we felt rejected us. Making direct amends and taking a personal inventory continues our progress in the program and helps free us from all the hurts of the past. We know now that we can't afford to think long about real or imagined hurts, or we will throw ourselves back into saddening ourselves once again. And any time we want to stop and reflect on how badly other people have treated us, we need to reflect on what we are doing to ourselves by all this negative rehashing. We are giving in to a compulsion that leads us down a path that is darkness, isolation and pain. The more we take an inventory of our actions, thoughts, and feelings, the more we will be forewarned about those thoughts that we previously had saddened our lives with.

Just the feeling that we want to withdraw from everyone is a warning signal that we need to get to a meeting, talk to a friend, and get moving. It is our efforts to face the risk of living with the unpredictable that will free us from saddening ourselves. *Depressed Anonymous* is not the place to have people feel sorry for you. *Depressed Anonymous* is a spiritual program where you will find people like yourself, honestly, openly and willingly dealing with their character defects and gradually admitting that they will have to change their lives and lifestyle if they are going to be a whole and honest human being. The decision is yours. You make the choice! The Twelve Steps and your own personal story can now be shared with others and can help them on their own life's journey.

The promises of *Alcoholics Anonymous* apply equally well to those who are working the same Twelve Steps in *Depressed Anonymous.*

"If we are painstaking about this phase of our development, we will be amazed before we are halfway through. We are going to know a new happiness. We will not regret the past nor wish to shut the door on it. We will comprehend the word "serenity" and we will know peace. No matter how far down the scale we have gone, we will see how our experience can benefit others. That feeling of uselessness and self-pity will disappear. We will lose interest in selfish things and gain interest in our fellows. Self-seeking will slip away. Our whole attitude and outlook upon life will change. The fear of people and of economic insecurity will leave us. We will intuitively know how to handle situations which used to baffle us. We will suddenly realize that God is doing for us what we could not do for ourselves. Are these extravagant promises? We think not. They are being fulfilled among us – sometimes quickly, sometimes slowly. They will always materialize if we work for them."

These promises indeed are true and we know they are true because of the witness of the thousands upon thousands of addicted people who are now free from their compulsions because of working the Twelve Steps everyday of their lives. Those people who have worked the Twelve Steps for any addiction imaginable have found that their compulsion has been defeated and they are recovering their very best selves.

I thank God every day for my freedom from my addiction, and I am now able to share my story of how God is working in my life with other members of the *Depressed Anonymous* group. My healing, like yours, is now being passed along to all those persons whose depression has made their lives un-manageable. With our new found belief in a Power greater than ourselves, we are living manifestations of God's power at work. **Thy will be done!**

Personal Stories

Members of *Depressed Anonymous* speak about their recovery from depression.

1. I no longer experience those black, bleak, hopeless periods. My life is joyful.

The blackness – the despair – withdrawing more and more into myself – the hopelessness – there was no joy and I could no longer pretend. My husband said: "You need to get some help." I knew that he was right but I was always the one who helped others. Our newspaper carried a listing of all of the support groups in the community and I found the notice for a Twelve Step *Depressed Anonymous* group. I had never heard of it before, but I knew it fit. The group was just forming and was there when I needed it.

I had knowledge of Twelve Step programs and actually believed that I lived that life. Today I know that I previously had head knowledge but today I live the Twelve Step life.

It was December of 1992 that I made that decision. I knew that I was powerless over depression and that my life had become un-manageable. I was willing to do anything that *Depressed Anonymous* offered. I wanted to get rid of the pain. If *Depressed Anonymous* had told me I would get well if I stood on my head three times a day, I would have done it. Daily, I read from the book and consciously worked the Twelve Steps. I worked them one at a time, from Step One through Step Twelve. Working the Steps to me meant posting the Step I was working on and consciously pondering it throughout the day.

Unlike other established Twelve Step programs, there was no evidence of recovery at these first meetings. The group was just forming. There was no one there with longevity in the program. The book gave me a formula. It promised me that I would feel better if I attended meetings, worked my Twelve Step program, ate properly, got an exercise program, and talked about my sadness to others. I also started a journal, not just to state my woes, but with the intention of finding a solution. Each week, I articulated my unhappiness and my story to people who listened, and over time, inner wisdom began to unscramble the mess.

Step Three ("Made a decision to turn my will and life over to the care of God, as I understand God") required much time, thought, and daily meditation. My Higher Power no longer was a permissive parent whom I begged to give me what I thought I wanted. All of the love, the caring, and the intelligence was there, I just had to accept it for myself. Today, the God of my understanding is different than when I began this journey. As a professional, educated woman, spiritually I was still in kindergarten. I badgered my counselor for a guide to assist me in taking my Fourth Step inventory. I wrote for months and then quickly moved to Step Five before I could rationalize it all away. The therapist who is responsible for beginning *Depressed Anonymous* in our area became another human being from our Fifth Step.

I no longer experience those black, bleak, and hopeless periods. My life is joyful. Then why do I continue to go to *Depressed Anonymous* five years later? The Twelfth Step of this program: "Having had a spiritual awakening as the result of these steps, we tried to carry this message to the depressed, and to practice these principles in all of our affairs." I am so grateful to *Depressed Anonymous* that I want it to be there for those who are still suffering.

The final situation that brought me to my knees and to *Depressed Anonymous* has not improved. In fact, it appears to be deteriorating. Our book says (in the section which discusses Step Six) that many would "no longer depress themselves if they could be sure there wouldn't be any more pain." No one can be promised a bed of roses without pain.

During my recovery, there were times when I would begin to interfere and I would remind myself of what it was like when I was attempting to run the show. Aloud I would say: "Oh I turned that one over to you and I trust you. I don't need to take it back."

Today I view the situation as "unfolding" and my spiritual journey is unfolding with it. My Higher Power is in charge.

-Lois

2. We never talked about our feelings.

My depression manifested itself throughout the duration of my childhood and teenage life. As an infant, I developed a fever of 105 degrees. This resulted in a series of learning disabilities because I developed a right cerebral dysfunction. I can remember the pain and trauma of being ousted by my peers because they thought I was stupid. This was because my speech and thinking was slow, and of course my grades validated that. I had to repeat the second grade because I didn't know how to read and my math skills were so poor. I had to be placed in several schools for disabled children to receive the extra help that I needed. Life at home was very dysfunctional. As a child, I noticed the lack of communication within the family. We rarely did anything together, such as a picnic and church. This was due to my father's general lack of enthusiasm for family activities and my mother's lack of experience. I was her only child. Neither of my parents were effective communicators and so I never learned to talk about my feelings. We were never settled down as we moved around constantly and I didn't learn how to make friends. Also, we didn't express feelings, not even much affection. The only sign of love that I saw between my parents was when my father was giving my mother a hug. That was after an argument and my mother had been sobbing and crying. Other than that, feelings (especially affection) remained withheld.

In 1979, when I was eight years old, my parents divorced. My mother entered a series of relationships, none of which were successful until now. I remembered the years I spend living in embarrassment, shouldering my mother's "dirty secret." I was living on a time bomb, waiting for it to explode and reveal the secret to the masses. What would happen if my peers ever found out? Would they throw stones at me?

In addition, a woman who decided to live with my mother did not like children and refused to see the good things about me. Anytime I made the least mistake, a discussion was raised. My faults were then served to me on a silver platter handed to me by this woman. I finally got the message that if I was to receive any approval; I had to be "perfect." That really makes sense!

So "perfect" I became. I stayed in my room and never played the stereo above a certain level. I didn't argue and did whatever I was told. If I went to my mother and tried to discuss my feelings about this woman, I was told: "She pays half the bills and you get to live here for free." Since no one took up for me, I quickly learned that I wasn't worth it. No matter how good and nice I appeared to be, I was bad, valueless, and worthless. I later learned the opposite. After my hospitalization for suicidal intent on October

1993, I joined *Depressed Anonymous*. I soon learned that people there loved me and that there were no conditions being placed on me to be "perfect." Other things fell into place. My mother and I became more like close friends instead of just parent and child. *Depressed Anonymous* really works!

There are other issues that must be addressed. I still need to learn not to feel bad if I make a mistake. Part of Steps Four and Five of *Depressed Anonymous* speak of not being afraid of being wrong and apologizing to the ones you have hurt. A flower does not grow unless you trim the weeds that choke it.

Depressed Anonymous had been the ultimate key to a largely successful life for me. Prior to entering the program, I had no money, no driver's license, and had dropped out of college due to poor grades and a nervous breakdown for which I was hospitalized. I had not then worked Step One because I wasn't aware that I was powerless over depression, that my life was as disorganized as the mess in my closet.

During my first night in the hospital, a member informed me of a support group known as *Depressed Anonymous*. I decided to give it a try. By telling me about this wonderful, miraculous, and very spiritual program, this person had not only worked the Twelfth Step, but had also given me a key, a key which would open many doors for me. Walking through these doors was like admitting defeat. I was playing first base in a ball game in which I would eventually win. If I struck out, I was back on Step One. By playing ball with a positive attitude, I was allowing my Higher Power to walk the Steps to recovery with me. With the help and the positive sense of fellowship that I enjoyed in the group, I began to understand God's will for me. With the love, support, and true friendship of three faithful members in the group, I began working on my driver's license, which had been another step towards independence for me. Within a year, I earned my license when two members of the group took me in for my road test. A new sunnier life had begun for me. The worst was finally over.

- Lena

3. I depressed myself. I can un-depress myself.

My name is Linda and the first time I read *Depressed? Here is a way out!* I did not like it and I got angry. The first part of the book about turning over our minds and life to a Higher Power sounded good. I was ready to do that. Hey! Here it is God! You take it! No more depression! But then came the part about a moral inventory, shortcomings, and the big one is that I depress myself.

"What's he talking about?" I said to myself as I read the book. I had tried to un-depress myself many times. I put the book down, and went to work. But as I was walking around at work that night feeling very depressed, bits and pieces of the book kept popping into my heard and I started to think of the word "stop" just like the book suggested to do. "I depressed myself, I can un-depress myself" I said to myself.

Look for SUNSPOTS, memories from the past that were happy times and ones which bring back happy feelings from years gone by. I tried, but none came to mind. But I did find that just thinking about the book and what it said did make me feel a little bit better. Then a piece of a song popped into my mind: "Seek you first the Kingdom of God and His Righteousness, and all the others will be added to you." "Hey! A SUNSPOT!" I said to myself.

Then I felt a warm glow and then I did feel better – I did it! I made myself feel better. I can undepress myself! I had mixed feelings. I wanted to feel better, but admitting I depressed myself was not an easy thing to do.

I went back and reread the book, but now with an open mind. I have started to follow the Twelve Steps and with the help of the Higher Power, I can have a brighter future. I am making and putting in my memory a lot of SUNSPOTS for those times when I am feeling depressed and which I can choose to draw upon when I feel that I need them.

I put up a "stop" sign and bring out a SUNSPOT to carry me through.

- Anonymous

4. Making gratitude my attitude helps keep Robin out of depression.

Through the *Depressed Anonymous* program, which utilizes the Twelve Steps, I have been on a journey of transformation from the familiar life of drudgery, gloom and desperation to discovering a new freedom and a new happiness – something I didn't know existed. My entire perspective is changing. Other people who I once thought were judgmental are now considered as all being a child of God – all created equal. What a peace provocative tool this is! Really! It helps me lift those negative attitudes and replaces them with affirmations. This is certainly the most valuable technique offered in *Depressed Anonymous:* to acquire an optimistic attitude towards life itself, or simply "making gratitude my attitude." So many of us were only familiar with the sham and the drudgery of life, but even with all the sham and drudgery in the world, it is still a beautiful place to live. We learn to change not the world, but how we view the world and all its intricacies.

Using the Twelve Steps allows me to begin the journey of hope and to admit that I am powerless over depression. There are times when depression overwhelms me so intensely that it nearly cripples me altogether. Those emotions of failure, shame and "feeling less than" become so uncontrollable that I have to stop and simply admit that I am powerless over them. But now I truly believe that there is a Power greater than myself and greater than those emotions.

This Higher Power (whom I choose to call God) is there to help me any time I ask Him. And you know what? He rescues me every single time!"

- Anonymous

5. The way it was and the way it is now.

I joined *Depressed Anonymous* in 1988. At that time, I was totally depressed, with no interest in anything or anyone, and especially no interest in myself. I felt that I had no worth, a feeling I had for many years, and I am sure since a child, very young.

Having lived with this feeling for so many years, I guess I thought this was normal, and probably most people felt the same way. I had all the symptoms of depression but I knew nothing about the sickness except to live with it. This was a terrible fate, until I discovered *Depressed Anonymous.*

I attend *Depressed Anonymous* meetings quite regularly. I have found that if I can attend the meetings regularly, I get the support of the members, who I have found to have about the same kind of problems as I have - maybe not quite as bad as mine, but I guess each of us feels that our problems are worse than anyone else. I know mine are. But with the regular meetings and my friends' support, I find that I am able to manage pretty well from week to week. I have more faith in myself since I work the Twelve Steps the best that I can and trust my Higher Power (God Almighty) with all my heart. I pray to the fullest extent that I will continue to have faith in myself and others. I have become a more whole being than I have ever been. I work a lot. I volunteer a lot and have a far better outlook on life than I have ever had. I attribute all of these good feelings to *Depressed Anonymous.*

I just hope that I will always be able to attend *Depressed Anonymous* meetings regularly and wish more people had the opportunity to do the same. *Depressed Anonymous* has helped me so much. I cannot begin to explain sufficiently the support the meetings can give one who is depressed. *Depressed Anonymous* has been and is my salvation. I know the Twelve Steps program is the only way to go to get one on the right track and it takes the meetings to keep you there. They are also a "Godsend" for me and I know for a lot of others who are depressed.

I thank *Depressed Anonymous* and my Higher Power for a life worth living.

- Frances

6. I was a compulsive over-eater.

Hi, my name is Linda, and I am more than glad to share what *Depressed Anonymous* has done for me.

I am the adult child of an alcoholic father and I seem to fit very well into the characteristics of the child of an alcoholic parent: guilt, shame, worthlessness, low self-esteem. I abhor alcohol to this day, but my addiction has become food. I am a compulsive overeater, having gained more than one hundred and fifty pounds in ten years. I am petrified by this. I had gotten to the point of withdrawal from everyone, was terrible lonely, and very depressed. I hit bottom. By this time I was feeling so worthless, hopeless and depressed that the thought of suicide was the only relief that I could find. What really scared me was that I almost found pleasure in these thoughts.

After all, there would be no more pain! But deep down inside, I really wanted to live. I love life and I want to live life to the fullest. But how? The depression just keeps coming and pushing at me, and a million negative thoughts that seem to completely overwhelm me at times.

Then a friend told me about *Depressed Anonymous* and I was so desperate that I went. To my surprise, these wonderful people accepted me, all of me, for myself. They encouraged me right from the start. They were open and honest about their pain and constantly reassured me that I could make it! But I would have to work very hard, because you have to really fight depression – negative thoughts replaced by positive thoughts - action to create motivation. Most of all, I had to surrender to God, quit controlling everything and everyone, including God. Let go and let God! So I started reading the Twelve Steps. At first, I was really rebellious, so much so that I didn't go back for two weeks. I was too depressed, but inside I knew the Steps had the key to get me out of this prison. They pointed me to my Higher Power, which unashamedly is Jesus Christ. Now I attend every meeting, sharing the things I learned and the times I fall (which are still quite a few) into depression. But it is working, and I could not be writing this right now if it was not for the love and the support of these very special people. As a matter of fact, I told them once a week was not enough for me. The leader suggested that I start another one, which is just what I have done. I now attend the meetings twice a week – twice is nice!

To sum it up, *Depressed Anonymous* has pointed to the only hope there is – our Higher Power is the only way out. Our Higher Power is the key, the life, and the hope. And once I have been able to admit that, everyone in the group has been very loving and supportive. After all, they have all been where I am today.

- Linda

7. *Depressed Anonymous* is Ralph's Guardian Angel.

I was thrown into my deep depression by the notice of our plant closing, where I had worked for 24 years. I felt my whole world as I had known it had folded in on me. I could not visualize my working at another place. I thought of all the negative things about starting over (my pay would be less, lousiest job, 3rd shift, first to be laid off, etc.). It went on and on.

This was just some of all the living hell that was going through me. But then my eyes and ears started to open through the *Depressed Anonymous* group. I just knew that God was speaking to me through them. He started letting me know that He hadn't deserted me or let me down. I knew that my life wasn't over, but going through a new phase, a new rebirth.

He told me that I must first forgive the company where I had worked for over 24 years. This was the greatest hurdle of all, but somehow I did it. From the moment I did it, my depression started to lift from my body. Next, he said that I must have faith in Him. He was going to take care of me and make me happier than I had ever been in my life. So He did just that.

I have a new job, which I love, and the pay is great! He said to quit bashing myself and to believe in myself and know that I can conquer all. But he never did ask me to forgive Him. Now I can understand why. There was nothing to forgive. My Higher Power knew what He was doing all the time. I believe now that I have become much closer to my God and have a greater faith in Him, namely, a faith that he will take care of me forever.

I have come a long way since that first day I walked through those doors and into all of your open arms. It was good to know that other people had the same feelings that I had experienced. I had feelings of loneliness and despair, and felt there was no way out of the living hell that was going through me inside. At that time, it was like my heart and my soul had been ripped out of my body.

I felt that my own mind was my worst enemy and its mission was to destroy me. I had many sleepless nights and my mind was forever racing with negative thoughts of gloom and doom. I did not think that I would ever function like a normal human being again. I felt my negative thoughts would win the battle and that I would forever be condemned to the eternal hell.

The *Depressed Anonymous* group has proven me all wrong (thank God). The group has been my guardian angel who was speaking to me all the time. I learned that there was hope for me after all. There is a new rebirth in me spiritually, emotionally, and physically. I believe now that I can go on with my life without all the fears that I bottled up inside me. As long as I have faith in my Higher Power and the *Depressed Anonymous* group, there will be no mountain that I cannot climb. I am forever grateful.

- Ralph

8. I couldn't get out of bed in the morning.

When I first came to *Depressed Anonymous,* I was so depressed. I didn't even want to get out of bed in the morning. I hated the world and I didn't want to deal with it. Just going out in public was a major ordeal - even the grocery seemed like an overwhelming task. Ultimately, I lost my job due to my inability to function at work. I prayed that God would let me die.

I felt as if I carried this tremendous load of emotional pain around in my chest all the time. I wanted to put it down. I wanted to get rid of it, but I didn't know how. I thought God had forsaken me because I violated some sacred code without knowing it. I believed that I would never feel the sunlight of the spirit on my face again. That belief forged a bitterness and resentment toward God that grew day by day. I could not believe that life would ever be good again, or that I could be happy. I felt emotionally dead. I have had depression for years, although I didn't know that's what it was. Being an alcoholic and an active member of *Alcoholics Anonymous*, I thought my depression and sadness were normal. I hit bottom last year in the spring, after eight years in recovery, when I started to have flashbacks of sexual abuse from childhood. I didn't understand how God could have allowed this to happen. Since it had happened so long ago, why did it have to come out now? All my life, I had this feeling that I had a deep dark secret, but I couldn't remember what it was. I lived in constant fear that people would find out that my terrible secret was out. Gradually, I realized that the big black secret was out now. I had not died. The world had not stopped moving.

As I began working on the abuse issues in therapy, the pieces of my life began to fit together in a way they never could have before, as I had never dealt with this catastrophic event. In the book: *Depressed? Here is a Way Out!,* he talks about how people find their time of depression to be one of the great gifts in their life. The first time I read this, I thought it was the craziest thing I had ever heard. Yet during this time of depression, I have learned and I have grown. I have come to understand myself and my God in a way I never could before.

It's been nearly a year now. Life is starting to come together for me again, one day at a time by the grace of God and the fellowship of this program. From the very first time I walked through the doors of *Depressed Anonymous,* I knew that I was in the right place. Having been an active member of *Alcoholics Anonymous* for so many years, I was already a firm believer in the Twelve Steps. I attended meetings; I worked the Steps with my sponsor. I used the *Depressed Anonymous* phone list and talked to people about my pain and my day to day problems. I read the book and followed the suggestions given in it.

With God, through *Depressed Anonymous,* this program and the fellowship literally carried me through the darkest time in my life and He did not let me die. I have truly experienced the "miracle of the group." I have heard it said that sometimes God's greatest miracles are unanswered prayers. I believe it. After all that I am one.

- Anonymous

9. A victim in my own mind.

Depression was something I grew up with. I really had no idea that I had it until my senior year in college. It started with my parent's divorce and ended with me totally losing control over everything in my life. I couldn't decide what career I wanted, but hated every job I could think of. I couldn't decide what city or state to live in, so I kept moving, hoping that the next place I lived in would make me happy. Eventually, I couldn't decide whether I wanted to live or to die. I cried at the drop of a hat, but still found enough rage inside to push the people I loved as far away from me as possible.

I knew that I needed help. I had been to counselors on three other times in my life, but nothing ever seemed to work or last. This time, I have been in counseling for about two months. I was sick and tired of being like this. I wanted a life and I wanted to be happy. Every week, someone would notice a change in me, but I still felt the same. Then one day while watching TV (thinking thoughts at 100mph), it occurred to me that I was making myself miserable.

I had always known that I was hard on myself. I reamed myself every time something bad happened. "Why can't I find someone to love me?" "Why isn't God looking after me?" But for some reason, when I realized that I was doing this to myself, it made me realize that maybe all I would have to do is stop doing it! All of a sudden, it made sense.

If I tell myself negative thoughts, I feel negative. If I tell myself nothing, I feel nothing. So if I tell myself positive thoughts, eventually I'll have to feel positive.

Of course, I'm still testing it out, but I feel better and for the first time in 14 years, I have hope. It's not that hard to find something positive about myself or my life now. So I remind myself of something positive every day and that's what I'm going to do until I don't have to remind myself anymore because I'll know.

I'm slowly finding out that my life is not as horrible as I've made it out to be. I used to tell myself that since it happened before, it will happen again – and that simply is not true. Yes, my past was horrible and it's no wonder I ended up with depression. I want out of it and the only person to get me out is me. There is not a magic wand to transport you to the life you want. Everyone knows what they wish their life could be like – so do it! Make the changes you have to make, trust in God and always remember that good things come to those who wait. I've waited over half my life. I don't have to be a victim of my past or of my mind anymore. I'm more than ready for the good things! With Love and Hope!

- A *Depressed Anonymous* member

10. I was sexually abused!

I don't remember ever not being depressed, even as a small child. My grandmother always said that I was too nervous. I was sexually abused and picked on in my childhood. I was picked on because my ears were too big. I was told that I was ugly and a substandard human being. I believed it. I was the butt of the jokes. I didn't feel like I was worth defending. I didn't defend myself against the neighborhood bullies.

Around the age of twelve, I began passing out. I was told by doctors that it was emotionally triggered but my parents did not believe it. I was into adulthood with these feelings of shame and inadequacies and even once attempted suicide, then after over twenty years of passing out, I hit rock bottom. I was tired of the strangle hold that depression had on me. I began therapy. I realized through therapy sessions that my fainting spells occurred during periods of personal loss, such as the loss of loved ones and the loss of my childhood. I am learning that I am worth saving from depression. What I think is important is what matters, ultimately. I will strive for recovery from my addiction to depression one day at a time. One day at a time will help me get over my depression. I will conquer my fears. I am a good person and I care about myself. I will resolve today to quit whipping myself over my past life. Today is all I have to make the most of and I plan to do just that.

- Steve

11. I am bi-polar (manic-depression) and found the *Depressed Anonymous* fellowship to be a miracle.

I was diagnosed as a manic depressive in 1981. I have been in therapy and on and off medication for approximately thirteen years now. Don't think that all that therapy and medication didn't do me any good. They say to take things one step at a time. I have taken some big and adventurous steps toward my progress with medicine and therapy.

But this year my progress has already surpassed all the past progress. It is because of my discovery of *Depressed Anonymous*. I call *Depressed Anonymous* a miracle. So far, the most grabbing element of *Depressed Anonymous* has been the parts in the book where the author refers to the depressed person as a saddict, that is, a person attached or addicted even to sad and hopeless thoughts. Boy, did I ever see myself in these sections. Since then, I have learned to control my thought process. Now, very seldom, do sad thoughts creep in. If I didn't know any better, I'd say the first time I saw the description of a saddict; a light went on in my head. The actual miracle took place at that moment. And the beauty of the whole thing is that thinking positive thoughts becomes easier and easier, automatic, then ecstatic at times.

But it is not all that easy. I followed the Steps also. I work at them often. For just as sure as your mind is on the automatic positive gear, it can easily slip back to negativism without the proper maintenance, which includes weekly (not just regular) attendance at meetings, and the knowledge and practice of the Twelve Steps as well as for those that need it, medication plus therapy as recommended by your doctor.

Good luck! And if just one other person reaches the point where I am, then there is a hope that life can be different for you as well.

-Julia

12. The more meetings I attend, the better I feel.

Like everyone else who had never done it before, I had no idea what to expect when I entered the room where a *Depressed Anonymous* meeting was about to be held.

I was instantly greeted by some women who introduced themselves by first name only and I responded with my full name. I didn't know if I'd broken any rules or not. I learned later that many newcomers do the same thing before they learn what's going on. I suppose it's because the idea of not giving your last name is so new that you just blurt out your surname without really thinking. I did feel like a stranger for a few moments as more and more people arrived and jumped right into discussion with the others.

But when the meeting started, I began to hear how other people's stories applied to me. I knew it was where I belonged. We each took a few minutes to talk about the proceeding week and how we fared.

I had just finished a series of outpatient group sessions at a hospital where we really spilled our guts and the other people gave their opinions and offered advice. Naturally, I spilled my guts. I didn't realize until everyone else had spoken that I really didn't need to tell everything. I also found that no one was giving me advice or being critical or prying. They were just willing to listen. I was aware that others were nodding in agreement at some of the things I was saying as if to say: "I know. I've been there," or "Yes, we understand completely."

I was somewhat surprised that some people cried as they spoke of their painful lives. I had a lump in my throat myself when I spoke. My heart leaped out to them immediately. I wanted to hug them and tell them everything was going to be all right.

I didn't really get the complete feel for *Depressed Anonymous* at that first meeting. I took the advice given to me as I was leaving and came back the following week. The more I attended, the better I was able to handle my depression. *Depressed Anonymous* did more for me in a month than the hospital group did in three months. *Depressed Anonymous* didn't cost anything (although after the first meeting, we voluntarily toss a dollar the end of each meeting to pay the light bill).

I couldn't believe that *Depressed Anonymous* was run by the people who participated in it. I thought there had to be someone, somewhere making big money off the poor souls who so desperately sought help. Boy, was that a stupid assumption. Perhaps the thing that has impressed me the most about *Depressed Anonymous* is the wonderful friendships that develop. *Depressed Anonymous* members really care about each other.

I thought that I had one personal friend outside my family. After I'd been to a few *Depressed Anonymous* meetings, I found that I had many friends, all caring, and most importantly perhaps, understanding.

Sometimes we go out for coffee after meetings and get to know each other even better. We occasionally have a party and find that we can be completely relaxed and at ease because there are people who absolutely understand each other.

We know what depression is all about in *Depressed Anonymous*. We know it takes the group to start to feel better. It may require medication and other things, but it absolutely requires *Depressed Anonymous*.

-Tom

13. I found that my drinking and depression didn't mix!

My mother had died in 1983 and I fell into a severe depression. I felt overwhelmed and suicidal.

I never actually attempted suicide because the alcohol came into my life. It dulled my senses and made me oblivious. Alcohol also at the same time gave me this feeling of empowerment and happiness, but at the same time, resentment – because I knew what was bothering me and didn't quite want to address the issue.

It wasn't until 1993 that I joined Alcoholics Anonymous and got into therapy, which has been amazingly helpful. I'm growing and dealing with the death of my mother and with alcohol. My hobbies, like gardening and my writing give me great joy and are therapeutic. I've been working the Twelve Steps with an open mind that every day things will get better. If a problem does occur, the Higher Power will give me the answer and the strength to deal with it, and not to run away or shut it away like before.

Depression is something that's so overwhelming. For me, it's like crawling from beneath the earth and facing the light with fear that no one would understand how I truly feel. When in depression, isolation would follow as my only friend, but actually, it was my own worst enemy. I should have been opening up to someone. Instead, I shut myself off from the world.

Through therapy, a belief in myself, and encouragement, facing each day doesn't seem as difficult.

Working my Twelve Steps of *Depressed Anonymous* and reading: *Higher Thoughts for Down Days* gives me reassurance that we are not alone. I now appreciate what I do have when I work through the program.

Through prayer and appreciation, I realize that there's more to life than alcohol and that I kissed a chunk of my life away because of it.

Now I'm gaining mush more through life than ever. Being sober, I see my life as a gift and not as a heavy burden.

- Rheatha

14. Today, two very depressed people called me for help.

As I sit here late at night, I think of the two people who called me today and who said that they are depressed. A man in his late forties and a woman in her late sixties are both troubled. They both feel alone and stuck. I talked with both of them and tried to get a fix on how much hurt they are feeling. How hopeless are they feeling right now?

I wonder if the lady will take my suggestions and go to her library and pull out a book I recommended for persons depressed. I wonder if she got out today into the beautiful warm autumn air. The gentleman said that he had recently lost a job and was out of work for a few months. Finally, he's back at work and he thinks things are a bit better for him.

I pray for both these folks tonight and wonder if they feel that maybe there is hope for them too? I wonder how I sounded to them. Did I actually promise hope? Did they really believe me when I said that their despair would lessen the more they came to our *Depressed Anonymous* meetings?

Depression is a horrible experience. I believe that it is truly a defense, as Dr. Dorothy Rowe claims. It is more a defense which many of us have learned how to use since our childhood days. It's more of a defense than a disease. Too often, persons depressed come to me and say that their depression really is a comfort because it protects them from something far worse than what they have.

They would hardly call a disease a comfort.

I wonder what goes through a person's mind when they learn that persons much like themselves are gaining strength from them. I talk with them about *Depressed Anonymous*. They seem interested. They tell me that they will attempt to make a meeting. They are hurting so bad that they are willing to learn and experience first- hand how being part of a group may give them a sense of empowerment and find it within themselves to gain an exit from the prison of their depression.

Empowerment and prevention are two realities that give us the push and the power for talking day after day with persons still suffering from depression. I know that some who hear about us will go with an expectant faith that they will find hope and peace in the group. This hope in itself may keep them from sliding down the slippery abyss of depression. Life is too short and the pain too great for our only life to be brought down by a pain so devastating. Only by sharing my pain can I ever hope to reduce its size. I wonder to myself if the man or the woman will be at any of our meetings tonight?

In a few hours the dawn will be upon me and another day will roll around. I wonder if my friends are worried, hopeful, or still afraid that their new day will be like all the rest. I wonder if they will pursue their hope and present their needs to our fellowship with its promise of a new birth and a new hope and new friends. I wonder?

It is with a personal sense of awe that I see the empowerment that comes to those persons who work the Twelve Step program of *Depressed Anonymous.* The empowerment comes to those who are conscious of the various ways they will have to change if they are to grow and change. This of course is not without its risks.

One of the major obstacles that we have to face when we are depressed is to be willing to change the way we think about ourselves, the world, and our future. To change the future, we have to dwell and experience the pleasant as well as the unpleasant feelings in the present. We have to be willing to face the discomfort of living life with a sense of unpredictability. This is not an easy task, but it is a task that can be achieved with time, patience and work.

Empowerment comes from being informed and making choices that help us change our lives for the better. When I come to a *Depressed Anonymous* meeting, I am making the first major step. I admit with my presence at the group meeting that my life is out of control. My compulsion to depress myself is at the root of my inability to take on the challenge of living life with risk and enthusiasm. But how can I possibly say that I want to depress myself? We are not blaming ourselves here but are taking responsibility for our own feelings, behavior, and thinking. Now that I am conscious of some, I can get on with learning new strategies for my own healing. With the heartfelt energy of a monk's prayer, I now understand that through sharing the story of my life and with the conviction that someone is there to listen, that this can in time help me make it out of my prison of fear and sadness.

I can be empowered by taking the bull by the horns and choosing to live one day at a time and start to feel differently. I now have the support from people who have walked where I am walking.

I am investing in myself. I am making my recovery the highest priority. I may have been on all the antidepressant medications and I may have seen all the best counselors, psychiatrists and doctors, but now finally, I am going to a room full of depressed people who understand me! These people I discover are investing in themselves. What will I find there? I will find some of the most caring people on the face of the earth.

Some of the group will have been coming for months. They say they are having more good days than bad, and it's getting better. The more meetings they attend, the better they feel and the more support they receive. They are feeling empowered. It's the miracle of the group. Instead of living with a compulsion to repeat old negative and life negating thoughts and feelings, we now have a compulsion to live with hope, plus a desire for a brand new way of living. We are now about to change the way we live and not just the way we talk to ourselves. We are going to get a life.

I now feel that I better understand how not to repeat my old way of thinking, feeling, believing, and isolating myself. I now know that this healing all takes time and that with work and patience, I will get better. For most of us, it has taken us a few years to get here (depressed) so why not take the time and daily work toward getting better one – one day at a time – one meeting at a time.

- Anonymous

15. My psychiatrist recommended *Depressed Anonymous*, now look at me.

My psychiatrist recommended *Depressed Anonymous* for depression. I began going to these meetings and obtained immediate support and acceptance. I cannot say enough for the Twelve Steps of *Depressed Anonymous* (and my weekly therapist concurs.) Neither can I say enough about the unquestioning acceptance I felt at my first meeting. They kept saying to attend six meetings before making a final decision. Well, I didn't need six meetings before making a final decision as to whether or not the meetings were for me. Since I lived about 25 miles away, I decided that a drive of that distance was a bit costly and inconvenient. My community doesn't have a group like this, and I'm sure there are many people in that area that can benefit from such a group. We had an organizational meeting with some key people from one of the existing groups, put our heads together and came up with good idea about how and when to proceed. The rest is history.

I have found the community as a whole is very supportive of this group. Individuals are a little reluctant to "come out of the closet" because of the stigma associated with depression. There is a tremendous amount of gratification that comes from helping someone that would not have otherwise known of this help.

Encouragement from someone else is essential. Even though you have an abundance of determination to make the thing work, it is very discouraging to attend a meeting and have no one show up. But thanks to a few stalwart believers in what I was doing, perseverance was encouraged and perseverance prevailed. Now I am happy to say that a strong close knit group exists. As a matter of fact, we're planning a chili supper soon and are looking forward to a night of socializing together. The tremendous rewards far outweigh the difficulties faced in the beginning. I highly recommend this to anyone who has a strong desire, determination, and perseverance.

I am going to be relocating to another area where there is no *Depressed Anonymous* group and I'm entertaining the idea of starting a group there.

- Barbara

16. A path of hope.

I think that most depression suffers go through a time of hopelessness and this feeling is very disabling for many of us. But with most problems or illnesses, there is always hope. Hope that our problem will be solved or we will get better. So if hope is part of the solution, how do we find our own path of hope? Before we take that path, I think it is important to see how the path is formed.

1). The first item is choices. We make choices every day for ourselves, some simple, and some complex. These choices may affect us for the rest of our lives: "What do I want to do in life?" "What do I want from life?" "What are my goals in life?" Our lives are formed and maybe our own meaning of what life is, is revealed to us. So our path is first formed with the choices that we make.

2). Next comes acceptance. Acceptance for who we are. Accepting our own ideas, values, feelings, and emotions. Even more important is accepting the fact that we can change our ideas, values, feelings and emotions. Accepting the fact that those changes can and will be made by ourselves and other people can't do that for us. They can only add to or detract from those changes. Accepting our choices and the responsibility for those choices. We have now begun our journey on the path of hope.

3). The third item is trust. Trust in ourselves to make the right choices. Trust in ourselves to overcome any obstacle we face, no matter how difficult it is. Also trusting another person, especially when that person loves, cares, or just believes in us. Trust is so important. It tells us that we are not alone and that we can accept and trust in another person to help us down our path as well as trusting in ourselves.

4). The last item is faith. Faith in ourselves that things will get better or problems will be solved even when no answer or solution is in sight or seems possible. Faith in others to help us when we need help and that they will be there for us. Faith in God or our Higher Power, and that because of our faith, our anguish, our sorrow, and our pain will be lifted. Faith in our path of hope.

The path of hope for depression sufferers is not easy to build or to find sometimes. That's why I think it is so important to take your medication, see your doctor, counselor or therapist and go to *Depressed Anonymous* meetings as often as you can. Remember, when all seems lost, there is always hope!

- Ray

17. There is a light at the end of the tunnel.

When I look at depression, I see long-term depression. *Long-term* depression as a result of a lost childhood, possibly from a lack of validation, love, trust, attention, abuse (sexual, physical or mental), or a loss of a significant person in your life. On the other hand, *short-term* depression has resulted in a major loss in your life (loss of a loved one, job, divorce – any major loss). Let me say at this point that I am not discounting any persons' feeling of depression.

I feel a *long-term* depression is less recognized by the person suffering from depression because the fact is that they have lived this way all their life and are addicted to depression. They feel that there is no problem. Depression is harder to work through because you have to reprogram your thinking. Motivation is essential but almost impossible. I find also that we are very controlling caretakers, or co-dependent. You have been comfortable this way and to change your thought patterns to let go of past hurts may seem impossible.

Short-term depression is just as hard to get out of but possibly easier to diagnose. A major loss in anyone's life can be depressing. Grieve your losses – don't shove back or stuff your feelings inside. Talk to someone. The more you talk about feelings and learn to trust your support group and the Higher Power, only then can you start to feel better.

As a person that has suffered depression since childhood, I can say that until you start to open up, share your hurts and feelings, listen to the members of the group, watch them as they grow from the support of the group, you will not be able to get out of the prison of your depression. I have been going to Depressed Anonymous for four years and only until recently have I realized that I was addicted to the self. Only then did I start to take a good look at myself and start to ask God for his help and truly mean it. I am learning to trust in God and do His will and not mine. I feel better about myself. I can tell you it is a lot easier to be depressed than it is to work on yourself and admit to yourself that there is a problem. It is God's will for us to live each day to the fullest because our time on earth is limited. Live each day, not yesterday or tomorrow. Share with the group and your friends and you will be surprised who will be glad to listen if you would give them a chance. Accept the fact that all of us at *Depressed Anonymous* are here to listen to you and not make judgments on you or give advice. Even if you don't want to share, come to the meetings because you can always get something out of them. Eventually, you will want to share and the group will listen.

In conclusion, trust in your Higher Power – God, as you understand God. Support groups are the way out of our addictions. We may have given up on God, but he hasn't given up on us. Start your day out by asking God: "God, I pray for the knowledge of thy will and the power to carry it out."

- Starr

18. Margie, a charter member of *Depressed Anonymous* shares her story.

I was asked to write an article quite some time ago, but I was still too close to the edge of getting over my depression to even want to "rehash" anything about it! I don't know when it really started and I don't know when it ended! I just know it has to be one of the worst experiences a person can have and it takes over our whole life. It makes us believe that life is not worth living. As I look back now, I believe my Dad suffered a lot of depression and it surely left its impression on me and especially my youngest sister, who has not overcome it yet and suffers mood swings and depression most of her waking hours.

I really can't remember for sure how I became involved in *Depressed Anonymous.* I believe a coworker told me about a professor at the University of Evansville who had students that were helping people in the psychology field and wanted to know if I would be a volunteer to help start this new self-help group. And it was free! What did I have to lose? I had seen doctors, took their prescribed drugs and still ended up on the same old merry-go-round of ups and downs and "hangovers" from the drugs. I joined a small group at first. We talked, set weekly goals, took short walks, visited with friends or enjoyed a cup of coffee to relax. We had to do something for ourselves. I had to learn to be good to myself, instead of nurturing everyone else. I found a good doctor who gave me a lot of good advice about "pampering" myself more. It hadn't been easy. I've read self-help books, positive thinking books and worked hard on my way of thinking for years. I'm a natural born worrier, so things always seemed worse than they really were. So after four marriages, I finally sat back and took a good look at myself. Why was I making these bad choices and keeping my head messed up? After staying single eight years and working on myself daily, I am now remarried and happy. I have two daughters, and two grandsons who are my pride and joy. I work with the elderly at a nursing home and manage to keep busy and happy.

After dropping out for several years, I'm now involved with *Depressed Anonymous* again. I feel like I have something to offer the group. Hope is the word. I finally got above the edge of the rut that I could barely peer over for years. I know others can do it too. Don't give up. It's a lot of hard work, but it can be done. I know. I was there.

-Anonymous

19. Is there life out there?

Before attending a *Depressed Anonymous* meeting, I honestly thought that I had nothing to live for. As a mother of five beautiful sons, a wife, and a mother to be of quads, I wasn't ever sure that I was a member of the human race. I couldn't eat, sleep, and cried for no reason. I wanted to be alone. It even got to the point that I didn't know who I was. I was a physical body without a life.

A black whirlpool of depression had sucked my will to live right out of me. That is really the only way that I can describe it. I was at the bottom trying to climb out. Everything was so far out of my reach.

Things happened during my pregnancy that I couldn't explain. I did things that I felt were right. My husband always thought that I was wrong. I couldn't please him and I couldn't even please myself. I couldn't make simple decisions. I would second guess every move that I made. There was one day – I couldn't decide if I should take a bath first and then iron my clothes. I honestly felt so stupid and crazy. I was afraid to go to the doctor because I thought that they would put me in a hospital and that I would never get out. I couldn't function on a daily basis. All I ever wanted to do was sleep and be alone. It got so bad that I would go to bed at night and pray to God that I wouldn't wake up.

During my pregnancy, my depression got so bad that I shut my husband completely out. My marriage was in trouble and I really didn't care. My husband and I constantly talked about divorce. I even waited a month to tell my husband about my pregnancy. I couldn't talk with my husband about anything. When I did try to talk, he told me that I was crazy or wrong to feel the way I did. He was always judging and preaching to me.

Then things started changing. My husband got a new job and we moved 70 miles away from our families. We still had all our old problems, but the move was going to make us dependent upon each other.

I would like to think that our move was a new beginning for us. I saw an ad for *Depressed Anonymous* on the television and called about it. It was my good fortune that there was a meeting that very night. I was so excited. I went to the meeting and it was such a relief to know that there were people out there that had depression just like me. I wasn't alone any more.

I've been going to *Depressed Anonymous* now for about five months. The program and my new found friends have been a miracle of God. So many people have a big misconception about our meetings. They think we all sit around, tell our stories and cry to each other's shoulders. Well, there's a news flash for them – we learn that each and every one of us has experienced some degree of depression in our lives. We find out how to laugh, comfort each other and sincerely understand what each one is going through because we have all been here at one time or another. We also learn that there is always hope. Since coming to Depressed Anonymous, I have learned to grieve for my lost children and how to live with my depression. I still have good and bad days. I am currently pregnant again with possibly twins. My husband and I are still working on our marriage, I now talk with him and it gets easier with time. My life is not perfect, but now with the love of my God, my family, my friends, and my husband, life is now worth living. But, the most important thing is that there is life after depression!

- Tommie

20. The power of Depressed Anonymous.

What is the power of Depressed Anonymous? Well, first let me say that when I started attending Depressed Anonymous meetings, I went for a couple of months and then stopped. I stopped going because my depression was so bad that I didn't want to leave my apartment. I didn't want to be around or talk to anyone. I just didn't want to do anything except crawl in a hole somewhere and isolate myself from everything. Then after about six weeks of isolation, I called the residential treatment facility where I had been a client to see if I had received any mail there and one of the members of the Depressed Anonymous group where I attend answered the phone. I spent a few minutes talking to her and there was something in her voice that told me that for some reason, it was important for me to be at the meeting. I attended the next Depressed Anonymous meeting. After the meeting was over, I suddenly realized the importance and power of Depressed Anonymous.

So what is the power if Depressed Anonymous? For me, it's just like attending that first meeting. I was a little scared and apprehensive at first, but then I found the Depressed Anonymous meeting was a place to go where there were other depressed people just like me. They could relate to and understand what I was going through. They didn't judge me or think of me as crazy. I was accepted.

Another power of Depressed Anonymous is the miracle of the group and what each person brings to the group. I have seen our fellowship get stronger and grow. I have developed many friendships that I can depend on for support and understanding. I have watched some of the newcomers that have kept coming back grow and improve. Even something as simple as a smile when there was none before. The miracle of the group empowers and energizes me.

The most important power of *Depressed Anonymous* is hope. Hope that we will not be locked in the prison of depression forever and that there is a way out for each of us. A hope that our Higher Power will work the miracle through us and that we will find our own happiness. I have hope that our hearts and minds will know love and peace like we have never known or felt before. The power of *Depressed Anonymous* works for me. I hope and pray that it works for you. Keep coming back!

- Ray

21. Today's Hope: *Depressed Anonymous.*

1 - Today I can experience hope. I will believe I can live this day with pleasant thoughts. I will do one activity that will give me hope and light for today.

2 – Today I will "not" dwell on the past and the losses that have occurred up until those times and space.

3 – Today I will "do" whatever I can to put movement into my life. Any small effort will help lessen the feelings of the stagnant sadness of depression.

4 – Today I will look forward to seeing a rose, the sunshine, a precious person – be it a baby laughing, a child at play, an elderly person on a park bench, and let myself believe that we are "all" of infinite value and very loved.

5 – Today I will embrace myself in some small way and this may be going to lunch with a friend or for coffee, or ice cream or a good brisk walk to the park or around the mall, or just a smile into my mirror back at me. I will believe that I am worthwhile and worth the effort to recover today.

6 – Today I will believe I can live this entire day "hopeful" and that I can return to the above activities anytime and as many times as I need to just for today.

- Mary

22. The "Miracle" of the Group.

The recovery program of *Depressed Anonymous* is similar to *Alcoholics Anonymous* and other Twelve Step programs in two important ways: 1 – You must attend meetings regularly, and 2 – You must have that vital spiritual experience that will change your whole life.

One recent American author speaks about the "three A's" in our society which determine whether you have "made it" or not: Affluence, achievement and appearance. Jesus says "If you want to make it with me, you must first die to self." His way is much different than the way of modem culture. To most, the cross is anathema!

The Bible talks about loving the self: "You shall love the Lord the God with all your heart and all your mind and all your soul and your neighbor as yourself." It was also said that "Love is the fulfillment of the Law." We know that we must first love ourselves if we are to love others. God dwells in the self. "We are the temple of the Holy Spirit" and "The Kingdom of heaven is within you," which is at least one of the reasons why we, as the depressed person, need to quit beating ourselves up when we speak of a Spiritual Awakening.

Many of us as depressed persons find it hard to trust God. As equally bewildering is the idea of trusting ourselves. In working the Twelve Steps and attending *Depressed Anonymous* meetings, I found that I can trust God. Gradually, I became aware that God loves me. I can trust God. Life is unpredictable and at times very difficult, but this new understanding that we have of God and who loves me greatly wants to give us all the good that we can handle. Once I begin to trust God who loves me unconditionally, then I might begin to love myself.

When we know our limitations, we know there is something greater than ourselves. In the Twelve Step program, this something greater is called the "Higher Power" or "God, as you understand God." I personally choose to call this Power: "God." I believe it cannot be less than personal, which is why I refer to my Higher Power as having a personal relationship with Jesus Christ. But the main path toward freeing ourselves from depression is to have some personal God. That God can be the God of our understanding. What freedom!

I have participated in many *Depressed Anonymous* meetings. I got to experience the "miracle of the group." In listening to other stories and in recounting my own personal trials, I became aware of what one author in a devotional meant in saying: "All your trials are gifts to you and opportunities to grow. You will not grow if you set in a flower garden. But you will grow if you are in pain, if you experience losses, and if you take the pain and learn to accept it as a gift with a specific purpose."

I met many people who were experiencing great losses and countless problems, but had decided to take action by attending a meeting to gain insight into their own lives. In my own grief, I became more aware of the suffering of others and began growing as a person. I had the opportunity to read at a *Depressed Anonymous* meeting where I shared my own experiences with depression and my complete recovery through reading the book: *"Depressed? Here is a way out!"* This book I believe was truly inspired by God.

Spirituality is emphasized in the *Depressed Anonymous* program, and through *Depressed Anonymous,* I feel I've become much closer to God, myself, and to others. I plan to continue my work with *Depressed Anonymous* by attending meetings and making contributions to The Antidepressant Tablet.

When I first became involved with *Depressed Anonymous,* I felt almost overwhelmed by the goals I wanted accomplished. I had been so inspired by the *Depressed Anonymous* manual that I wanted to do everything I could for the people at *Depressed Anonymous.* Through experience, my own personal vision became that of Mother Teresa of Calcutta who said: "There are no great acts, only small acts done with great love."

-Nealia

23. To be depressed or not be depressed? That was my choice.

I believe I've been a depressed person all of my life. I've had a lot of lows but never as low as this past year. My husband of ten years left me and my three children for another woman. I lost my job. Depression hit me and I couldn't snap out of it. My life started to spiral down. I was in and out of mental hospitals and on different medications. I was diagnosed as having a chemical imbalance. In my mind, this seemed to tell me that I had a sickness that I had no control over and which only drugs could cure. Then one night, I began to have a horrible reaction to the last drug. I was rushed to the emergency room and almost died. After that, I refused to take drugs again. Then life really started going down for me. I started sleeping more, stayed in bed mostly, and let the house and the children go. I felt empty inside. No one or anything could help me. If I hadn't thought suicide was the cardinal sin, I would be dead today. So one night, I lay on the floor crying and praying from my heart. In the past when I prayed, I wanted God to do all the work. While deep down, I still didn't want to let go of my miserable, yet safe way of life. And as long as I wouldn't really let go, God seemed to have no answers for me. This time though, I was at his mercy. Life for me could no longer go on this way. I prayed the most releasing prayer. I offered up my entire self to him. Nothing magical happened after that except the sudden urge to call my church for Christian counseling. They referred me to this very affordable, warm lady counselor who I had seen in the past. She suggested that I start attending *Depressed Anonymous* Twelve Step meetings. This was a great effort for me. I was scared and skeptical. Since that first night, I've been attending weekly *Depressed Anonymous* meetings and reading: *Depressed? Here is a way out!* I also attend drug free therapy, attend church and church activities regularly and continue to pray and walk regularly. I know that my life is being richly blessed. I'm also using the *Depressed Anonymous* literature and listening to people in the *Depressed Anonymous* meetings where I received valuable tools which I put to daily use.

The moment that I read that I had a choice to stay in depression, I immediately knew that I could make the choice to get out of my depression. Bingo! It wasn't an illness. This did not have control over me. And another tool I use frequently through the *Depressed Anonymous* manual is that "thoughts produce moods, moods produce feelings, and feelings produce behavior."

So I began to realize that if I thought about sad or disturbing thoughts, I could stop myself and produce positive thoughts automatically. I had control. This is priceless to me. Staying out of depression takes work on my part, as well as God's. Thank you Lord above for using people through my church, my therapy, and the wonderful *Depressed Anonymous* members who give of themselves unconditionally. Thank you for answering my prayer.

- Kim

24. *Depressed Anonymous* is my depression relapse prevention program.

For those of us who have ever spent some time in the desert, we know how important it is to carry water with us. Also, the human body cannot survive long without some form of liquid nourishment.

I have discovered an interesting fact in these last ten years as I have sat in and participated in hundreds of *Depressed Anonymous* meetings. The interesting fact is that depressed people begin to see that their depression is something that they feel they have to hang on to. They have to hang on to the depression because they are afraid that if they are no longer depressed, that nothing can take the place of the pain and despair of their depression. It's much like the depressed person who has to give up the comfort of that isolation and the feelings that accompanies the absence of those familiar thoughts. They are afraid that they will end up being the hole in the donut and a virtual cipher.

When we talk about depression and the many who experience it, we understand that much like other addicts, they too are filled with the terror of ending up as the hole in the donut once they abandon that comfortable and familiar feeling that we know as depression. In their discussion of depression, the members of the *Depressed Anonymous* group, especially the new members, will tell how their depression has been a big part of their life for so long and they are afraid of "letting go" of what has been familiar and predictable. They cannot and will not let go of this constant and familiar companion. They cannot give up something that they have had all their life and get something back which will probably be far worse than what they have presently. If they do risk trying to feel differently, the good feelings might last for awhile. But deep down, they know (without any basis in fact) that they will end up with all the old feelings of guilt, despair, and isolation. They also believe that even if things did get better for awhile, things would gradually sink back into that old familiar pit of hopelessness and despair. As Dr. Dorothy Rowe points out in her book: *Depression: The Way out of your Prison*: The depressed person has this immutable belief that since "bad things have happened to me in the past, bad things are bound to happen to me in the future." The depressed have to have complete certainty for their life because without it, it means that they must take responsibility for their lives and live life with risk and uncertainty. We know that there is no life without pain and uncertainty. The depressed imprison themselves with their own beliefs about their world. The meaning that they attach to that which happens in the world either can provide freedom or imprison them.

I hear this type of thinking expressed week after week at *Depressed Anonymous* meetings. I know that this type of thinking is how the depressed give their world and life meaning. This is how they make sense out of their existence. One's language does indeed create one's identity and reality!

When these same people who have learned how to sabotage themselves just as they begin to feel differently, they do this because they are afraid of what lies in store for them when the pain that they have felt for most of their lives is gone. These people cannot afford the risk of living with hope. If everything is for certain, then the reality of hope is superfluous. To live without certainty on a daily basis is to live with the unpredictability of life. And so in a terrible form of logic, they have conditioned themselves to see their personal world dark and gray without hope, lest it change. Change means that they would have to change. To live with change and the ramification of change means that I would have to take responsibility for my life, for my own feelings and the day to day adventure of living without certainty. Some would call this the adventure of living. I would rather go and withdraw and hide out and isolate myself from all those persons and situations that demand that I risk living in relationship with others in hope.

Despair, even though it may be fatal for some, is a state of safety and predictability for the depressed. In our groups of *Depressed Anonymous,* we can tell others that it is common to all of us to fear change and the uncertainty of living. But we must change if we want to free ourselves from the chains of depression.

When I hear of a severely depressed person begin to relate how he or she is afraid to let go of their sadness, I feel that these people are now willing to get better. They have had the honesty, willingness, and openness that is essential if they are to live lives of freedom and hope.

Depressed Anonymous happens to be the best arena for working through those times of uncertainty and attempt to live life without the hollowness, jitteriness, and pain. The fellowship will support you through this scary time of change as you develop the new you, filled now with friends and tools learned from the experts, who are fellow sufferers of depression.

- Anonymous

25. *Depressed Anonymous* provides a secure (love and acceptance) base for those who never experienced love or support while growing up.

After ten years of repeated meetings with the depressed of *Depressed Anonymous* meetings, it's clear that the meetings create a secure base for those who in their childhood had neither kindness, nor the life-giving warmth and affection of a loving family.

People who keep coming back to *Depressed Anonymous* continue to grow and become aware of the inner change taking place week after week as they find not only attention to their story, but find that they are loved and cared for at the same time. Possibly for the first time, they find that they look forward to each weekly meeting and become attached to the positive feelings that emerge inside themselves as they continue to share the story of their pain. In time, they share how their week is suddenly being filled with more good days than bad. It also becomes obvious to the participant that childhood behavior and experiences are carried right on into adult life. Trusting is such a hazard for the depressed because every person is different. You can't trust your environment because it could suddenly shift and you would be without a certainty that you were bad and worthless. The meetings gradually present to you an opportunity to be someone worthwhile and valued. Your sharing and risking information about yourself begins the construction of a new and secure you. The *Depressed Anonymous* group becomes for possibly the first time in your life, a very secure and stable environment where you can share, trust, and grow.

- Anonymous

26. In helping others, I helped myself.

I remember my first night at a *Depressed Anonymous* meeting. It was the 6th of June, 1985. I went into the room of people I didn't know and was afraid. I wondered what it would be like and sat at the back so I could leave if I wanted to. I was withdrawn with the pain of depression, so I knew I wouldn't open my mouth to these people I didn't know. The man in charge took me out to another room and asked me a few questions. I found out later it was to see if I needed medical care. When it came my turn to talk at the group of nine people, I refused. Everyone had a very sad story to tell. When I came home, I decided that I didn't need to hear any more sadness, so I wouldn't return the next Thursday night. I didn't. However, the next Thursday, I was ready to go try again.

After my fourth Thursday, I opened up a little. I didn't trust these people yet. As the Thursdays passed, I became more relaxed and realized they could become good friends to me. I felt a closeness to these people and I've always liked helping others, so I opened up more and more.

After meetings, we would to a restaurant for coffee and food. One night, I was laughing and talking, and our counselor in charge said: "Gloria, you have opened up like a rose. Petal by petal, you have opened up." Well, I felt special and very good inside. It had been a lot of work, and it was noticed by him. I felt proud.

I've gone through a lot of heartache these last five years. Eye surgery, mother's death, my grandson's wreck, husband's death, and I'm in the process of bringing my grandson back from the hell of drugs, alcohol, and Satan.

I moved to Evansville ten years ago. It is hard to make friends in a new city. But through my support groups at church, I have made lots of friends, super friendly people.

Depressed Anonymous is now meeting at a church. I'm a facilitator when I am needed. Something I never thought I could do five years ago. I pray before I go to meetings and ask God to speak through me to help these people. I always go to a new person, as I vividly remember my first meeting, and make them feel welcome.

There are four of us who were there together first on June 6, 1985. We have become very good friends. I still remember the things the counselor from the very first meeting told us. I've seen people come and go. Some helped, some for just one meeting, some wanting a magic wand waved. It has helped me over the rough spots, and gave me courage to go on as a widow. I have found a peace in life, a special joy in knowing and loving people. In helping others, I have helped myself. I know my background in life has made me depressed at times. My mother was abusive and I realized later in life that it was an emotional illness. I forgave her.

I will continue to attend *Depressed Anonymous.* Every meeting is different and who knows what mystery each group holds? One never knows who needs me, who needs a smile or hug, who needs to feel that they are not alone, or who needs to know that there is a God who loves all.

- Gloria

27. Sue's Story (Faith does Move Mountains).

Probably my earliest memory is one of depression. I remember getting a spanking from my father (I don't remember what for) at about the age of two or three years old. He kept on whipping me because I was crying and sniveling. I thought he would kill me because I kept on sniveling and couldn't stop. He said he would keep it up until I did stop. I quickly learned that crying and any other expression of emotion was a "no-no."

In my family, people did not cry, laugh, smile or show any emotions – above all, not love. We were also superior to other people. We were more intelligent, wealthy, over achievers, and elite. We ever carried the British "stiff upper lip" to new heights. Many people commented on my mother's beautiful face. She is eighty years old now and still has only a few wrinkles. Her beauty secret is staying out of the sun. She never sweats or goes places were there just might be "common" people, and never shows any emotion.

I only saw my father kiss my mother once. It was a brief, cold peck on the cheek as she was being wheeled off to surgery. I was an only child. My father was an alcoholic. My mother may have been one. My father had wanted to be a doctor and was very disappointed that I was a girl. He made no secret of it. I can remember when I was told that I would be a doctor. In my childhood at Christmas, I always got a doctor's kit and never one for nurses.

My family did not do things together such as picnics, attending ball games, or movies. If I went anywhere, it was with a girlfriend's family, or my father drove and picked me up afterwards. The only thing my family enjoyed was food, and we are all overweight.

In school, I made good grades in kindergarten. I got an "unsatisfactory" for talking too much. My father told me that if I got another "U," I would get beaten with his razor strap. When I got another "U" in conduct, I started crying and the teacher asked me why. When I told her, she erased it and said it was a mistake. When my father saw the report card, he thought I had erased it and I was whipped anyway. I quickly learned that I had a job earning good grades so that I could get into medical school. It was hard for a woman to get into medical school.

At the age of sixteen, I fell in love for the first time. He was a few years older. He had been in the Navy. He was clever enough to sit and listen to my father talk for hours about hunting and fishing. We broke up because he insisted on running away to get married. I knew that I had to finish high school. I was so depressed that I really wanted to die.

I met my husband to be when I was a senior in high school. We met in a church at the Christmas Eve candlelight service. He was handsome and very polite and well mannered. After awhile, we became sexually active.

In my senior year at high school, I decided that I wanted to be an engineer and design household appliances with features and conveniences that women would appreciate. I visited the dean of the local university and talked with him. He was enthusiastic. I came home excited and proud. Imagine the angry fit my father had when I told him. He told me that he would not pay one penny of the tuition unless I went to medical school.

I became more defiant after I entered college (pre-med). I got married at the age of eighteen, quit college and moved to Florida with my husband, Fred. We weren't able to earn a living in Florida, so we came back to

Louisville. After we were married a year, my first daughter was born. I noticed that Fred was drinking heavily on weekends. It progressed to every night. At least he went out to drink and didn't do it at home like my father. When I was pregnant with my second daughter, I found out that Fred was having an affair. I became very depressed and we separated. All during my marriage, my family pushed me to divorce him. I forgave him, but he continued drinking and was never at home. Finally, after ten years of marriage, he got a young girl pregnant. I realized that he was not a real father to the children anyway. I divorced him and went back to live with my parents.

I had worked for a doctor who was much older than me and who was highly respected in the community and in his church. He was a real father to me. He paid my college tuition for me to attend night classes. I was studying to be a CMA (certified medical assistant). I completed the college courses shortly after the time of my divorce. While going to college, I was working and dating someone I really cared about. He was transferred out of town. The doctor I worked for was giving me amphetamines. I would sometimes go for days without sleeping. I was really taking them a lot to keep going. He gave me sleeping pills. I didn't realize what this was doing to me. When I got my divorce, the doctor made some strong sexual advances to me and I quit my job. I had to go to Lawrence, Kansas to take the certification test. I was so depressed about the divorce, the doctor's advances, my loss of the boyfriend and my job. I thought I had failed the test. I was the first person in Kentucky to pass. I deliberately overdosed on sleeping pills and alcohol in my motel room in Kansas. The man in the next room heard me when I collapsed. The management called an ambulance and I recovered.

My family was so severe with me when I lived with them. This time, I was working for another doctor and had read the "perfect" way to overdose in his medical journal. My mother heard me when I fell down the stairs and I awoke in a psychiatric ward. At least the psychiatrist knew that I loved animals. He told me that my taking amphetamines were like beating a dying horse, so I quit taking them forever. I had shock treatments, which didn't help my depression and filled me with extreme fear of further treatment. I came out of the hospital to face all my old problems of trying to rear two children with little income, no family support or love. The doctor I worked for this time had fired me, and I had a hard time finding another job. I finally got one as a medical transcriber at a hospital. This was better because there was less contact with people. I could never trust working for a doctor again.

I continued this occupation for about twenty-five years. I had bouts of severe depression and was always somewhat depressed. I was mostly a recluse after my children were grown. But I thought this was all there was to life and I really had no hope of anything different. I had tried some antidepressants, but had such severe side effects that I could not take them.

As if this was not enough, in May 1989, I came down with a virus that caused brachial plexopathy and could not hold my arms up to type. I became disabled. I found that it would take months before I could begin getting disability payments. I quickly went through my meager savings and was in terror of becoming homeless, since my family would not help me.

I had started counseling, but my dear family thought I needed medicine (and probably hospitalization). At their insistence, I went to a local free clinic. The psychiatrist put me on a certain drug and after three days, I felt myself becoming really aggressive (I could have hit just about anyone), but I realized it and quit. I definitely feel this drug should be taken off the market. The psychiatrist at the clinic then put me on another drug, which made me want to sleep all the time. At the group sessions, I immediately saw that the members all looked and acted like zombies. They told me to keep coming and I would get better like they were. For activities, they strung beads and made muffins. One good look at them, and depression (or even suicide) did not look so bad.

About this time, a *Depressed Anonymous* group was started and I went to a meeting. I learned that the other members had the same problems, some had attempted suicide, but they were getting better and without being drugged into a stupor. I had always believed in Christ, even though my family did not attend church. I really thank my Higher Power for leading me to the church where my counselor attended. Here the Priest says that God loves us just as we are (not if we will change or be something else). The congregation is a very loving and supporting one, and so this made following the Twelve Steps easier for me. It was no trouble for me to realize that I was powerless over depression and that my life was un-manageable (Step 1). By looking at the faces and talking with the other members, I could see that they had obtained peace (Step 2). From there, Step 3 – turning my will and life over to the care of God – was easy. I just pictured myself struggling in the water. If you stop struggling in the water and just give up and lie on your back, you will float!

Action does precede motivation and I began working at a local zoo. It is a beautiful place (and safe from muggers too). I began talking with people and learned about classes there to become a docent (volunteer teacher). I enrolled and graduated. This gave me a new purpose in life. I get great joy from working there doing outreaches to schools, nursing homes and hospitals. I have made friends with both animals and humans. There isn't a day that I go there to talk that I don't get thanked by someone, a visitor, or employee (or sometimes an animal).

My family hasn't changed (although my mother commented on the change in my face), but I have. In this, the Serenity Prayer really helps. I know that I can't change them, but I have new friends and a real support system so this doesn't matter so much now.

Whoever you are, you who are reading this: Believe! The first Three Steps are the most important. Walking or other exercise is important. Staying with it is also important. Going to the meetings and participating is important, but above all else, faith is important. Faith will truly move mountains!

- Sue

28. I have to take responsibility for my own life.

I remember being very sad when I was very young. I really didn't understand that the sadness which I always experienced was called depression. I was sad as a child. I was not too happy to be living. I felt that I was never quite good enough to compete in school. I always felt that I should leave to someone else whatever we were doing. I suffered on and off with depression throughout school. I felt that I had a loving family, but there was always that depression.

When I went into adulthood, I was always determined to be in control. I had a great need to be in control. I felt weak if I wasn't in control. I guess I thought that if I wasn't in control, complete control, then the feeling that I wasn't quite as good as someone else would pass. I was never satisfied with what I would do. I always thought that I could do better. I was taught to do as well as I could. I guess I was my own worst enemy, but I never expected that from others. I always thought other people were okay. I expected so much from myself.

That inner battle and the depression went on. I could always sit down and talk with my mother. She made life so simple. After she was gone, I completely fell apart. I got more and more depressed. I didn't go out and find help because I was too scared. At first, I didn't know if there was anyone who could like me. How could they accept a person like me? Somebody had to accept me the way I as or nobody could help me.

My children were all married and had left home. I was divorced from my husband. I would come home to that empty house. I wasn't interested in anything. I didn't like television, radio, the video, or anything that made a sound. I just wanted to sit quietly in the corner. At the time, I didn't realize that I was doing this. I was thinking of all the old, negative thoughts that were making me so sick. I was not sleeping very much and had chest pains. That went on for a long time, but I didn't really care what was wrong. I would think to myself: "You are a worthless person anyway, always have been. Don't go to a doctor and take up his time, you're not worth it." Daytime at work was okay, but at nighttime, I would sit in the dark. It was somehow a comfort, and it felt good at the time. The only thing I could think was how I made a blunder on the job. "You could have done this or done that at work." I kept telling myself I should have been more friendly on the street to an acquaintance. I kept beating myself over the head about the things that happened a long time ago. I got to where I wouldn't see people. I would smile at people who came to my home and tell them that I was fine and couldn't be better. You weren't supposed to be rude to people who came to your home. If they find out who I really am, and what I really am, they will discard me completely. If I could tell all this to someone, but why tell it to anyone? Who wants to hear it?

Then I finally knew after two years or more of sleepless nights that someone had to help me. I found a card saying "Depressed Center" in the back of the phone book. It had a phone number and that was all. I talked to the man on the other end of the phone. I said to myself: "This man is too busy to talk with me," but anyway, I made the first appointment myself. I made myself go. I thank God that I did. I thank God that I went for help. It was a whole new beginning for me. I wanted to get well so badly. I think people do have to want to change. I went in with the attitude that I have to get well. I heard things about counselors that scared me, but this was just all the old negative feelings that caught up with me and boxed me in. I got better and started to think differently. I started to get rid of some of my negative thoughts. I began to feel better and I continued to see my counselor. I started in *Depressed Anonymous* some weeks later.

It has been a year now since I gave up on those negative thoughts that I had over my lifetime. I gave them up one at a time. It wasn't like I dumped them all at once. It was like the people needed to show me a new life and that I can be happy again. In the beginning, I thought the old familiar tapes had begun playing again. The old tapes saying that I was "stupid" began to play. But then I would attend *Depressed Anonymous* meetings every week and I would go and find that I could use things that other people said at the meetings which would help me. That it was one place where you could go and be fully accepted for whatever you had to say, and someone else there said that they knew exactly what I was feeling. I also began to trust in God as my Higher Power. More and more, I turned it over to the Higher Power and said I can't do these things all by myself. I did pray as hard as I could. I prayed every night. I believed that this change was going to happen. I started believing in me. But the wonderful thing was that I began to realize that I was no longer alone. A Higher Power was going to be there for me. The chest pains soon subsided and I began to sleep again.

You don't get better overnight, but you do get much better. I was as down in the muck as far as I could go. I had to go and open the door for the first time because there was no other place to go. I had already used up all the hiding places in my life. I still have many problems like anyone else, but when I need sleep very badly, I turn the problem over to the Higher Power and go to sleep. I can always pick life up the next morning. Somehow, it all gets done. Nothing so bad has happened to me. I have trouble trying to figure out what I am exactly supposed to do. I am sure God points me in the right direction. Sometimes, I miss the message, but it will come to me eventually what God wants for me. All you have to do is reach out and get it. But my faith is stronger now in God than it has ever been in my life because I need that companion in my life. It is there for all of us if we just reach out and take it.

Now that I look back and see the way I was and see how I am now, I can't believe that I ever knew that other person. This person is different altogether. I like this person now very much. I am so thankful to the group. They are just wonderful. They are my family. They are my *Depressed Anonymous* family. I also have my church family. It is a wonderful feeling to know that there is a Higher Power that can help you through these things. At first, I thought: "I doubt that very much" when everyone was talking about the Higher Power and peace in my life. Then it happened to me. Every few days, the world dumps down on you and beats you down. That's just life. I always think to myself that there is that extra strength that I didn't have before. I feel that everything is going to be OK with me. I have that peace now myself.

It can't happen overnight. I know what the people who come to *Depressed Anonymous* for the first time feel. When you go through the long weeks and days and give it all you got, it will happen to you just as it happened to me. There is no magic cure. There is no magic pill. It is a long process. It will happen and does happen. It is so much better than staying in that dark hole and not getting anything out of life. No longer could I blame this one or that one for causing me pain. I know that it was me that was beating myself up. I was unequipped to handle the problems of my life without the Higher Power, without the tools and material to build the better life.

I also had to get my priorities straight. I put a lot of importance on things that were not important, or what somebody else might say about me. I was afraid to change. I was afraid that I would change into a person that would be selfish and uncaring, but it didn't happen that way. I just found a different way to go about it. In getting my priorities straight, I discovered that if a person doesn't accept me the way I am, then that doesn't matter. I am going to do the best I can. If someone else can't handle that, I am awfully sorry about that, but it has to be. I want everyone to approve of me, but I am just not going to do that. I am not going to please everyone. I have got to take care of myself. I was so busy trying to please everyone else that I wasn't taking care of my own needs. At the time I was doing it, I didn't realize that I was doing it. Now I won't deliberately hurt anyone else, but I am going to take care of myself.

- Helen

29. I am no longer alone!

I am writing this information with the hope that it will help anyone who is suffering from depression that is brought on by stress, anxiety, loneliness, physical or mental emotions, death, or insecurity.

I am a thirty-four year old single female, who has been suffering from depression for a long time. Most of my depression was brought on by feelings of insecurity, such as not being able to express my inner feelings, being controlled by a dominating parent, loneliness, stress, workaholic, anxiety attacks (related to work and everyday pressures of living), too much sleep, nervousness, lack of motivation, being tired all the time, sadness, weight gain, digestive problems, a feeling of being trapped, self-consciousness, not trusting myself, dreams of dying but yet managing to come back to life, withdrawal from family, or loss of interest in meeting with the opposite sex.

It seemed that I was living in another world until one of my parents gave me a phone number of *Depressed Anonymous*. The *Depressed Anonymous* meetings, plus reading the *Depressed Anonymous* manual have provided me with the tools to live without being depressed. Most important of all, the Twelve Steps mentioned in the book have made me understand that God (my Higher Power) will give me strength to deal with my depression and get on with my life and be happy with myself.

The book, with its Twelve Steps, has taught me that I am not alone. And that I am not the only one who is suffering from depression. It has taught me to believe more in my Higher Power and to let it handle my depression.

I read the *Depressed Anonymous* manual, go to counseling, and attend the *Depressed Anonymous* meetings. The meetings are a must. I need them to survive. The support group's members help each other by listening, talking, expressing their feelings, and give support on how to cope with depression. By letting my Higher Power help me, I am beginning to feel free from depression. I am not so nervous and tensed up. My Christian inner faith is getting stronger. I am not so stressed out and I am beginning to get confidence within myself. I still have trouble with sleep pattern and I am getting some motivation back. I have learned how to handle anxiety by taking deep breaths when I am nervous or troubled. This was suggested by my therapist. I also am learning how to stand up for myself.

All these new tools have helped me and will continue to do so. They also taught me not to dwell on my past, to live life one day at a time, and to look toward the future, but not live there. It will take me a long time to deal with depression, but I am glad that these tools are available. Life can be good for a change. Please don't give up.

- Anonymous

30. *Depressed Anonymous* saved my life – twice.

Depressed Anonymous has saved my life twice now. When I first came, I had been suicidal for some time and was only looking for the right time and place to make it look like an accident. After a few meetings, the suicidal feeling began to leave. I started to realize that I wasn't the only one who was having problems coping with the problems of life.

This spring, I suffered from another bout of severe depression and had decided to end it all. I had the date, the approximate time, the place, and the accident all picked out. I started withdrawing from the *Depressed Anonymous* group so that they would not try to talk me out of it. I stopped taking my medication to make sure that I could not pull myself out of it. Our

Higher Power had different ideas. *Depressed Anonymous* members for some reason kept in contact knowing something was not right. That added a great deal of difficulty in carrying through with my plan because I could not distance myself from people who cared and showed it. It was very hard to know that I would be letting them down.

I managed to make the appointed day and had prepared to leave the house. As I said, the Higher Power had other ideas. Just before I left, a *Depressed Anonymous* member called me to just chat about themselves. That took a little time. Then all the neighbors, one after another, kept coming over to ask me to help them with little projects. It was very hard to put on a "happy" front, but I knew I had to do it or somebody would figure out that what was about to happen was not an accident.

By the time everything was done, it was dark and too late to leave. If I had left after dark and had the accident, it would have been obvious it wasn't one. This was a 400 foot high bridge in the middle of the wilderness that no one but emergency vehicles goes across after dark. The day ended and I was still alive and angry that my goal had not been accomplished. Now I would have to plan for another day.

Depressed Anonymous members came to my rescue again and through their support and listening, I finally overcame the deep depression. I am getting better each week. I know that if *Depressed Anonymous* had not been there for me that I would have continued on with my suicidal plans. I still get depressed. Sometimes I get very depressed, but *Depressed Anonymous* is there and it is the vehicle that the Higher Power is using to help me cope and learn how to "knock down this fire within me."

- Ron

31. Bill has two degrees behind his name and he still got depressed.

I became an active member of *Depressed Anonymous* after seeing my counselor for three or four months. I never knew that I was depressed. I never understood. I knew that I needed to make changes in my life. Many depressed people have this trouble, namely not being able to admit that something is truly wrong in their lives and that they need to change.

I started to realize that I was depressed seven or eight years ago. It started after the breakup with a girlfriend. I was devastated. I had good friends at work. I am well educated, with two degrees after my name, but I wasn't fulfilled. My world was falling apart. I lost two jobs. I lost my girl. I wanted to be left alone. The burden was too unreal. I didn't want to get up in the morning. I just wanted to be left alone to be isolated and bored. It was tough. I was nasty and mean. I sometimes still behave like this. I get angry and I get frustrated and get upset with myself.

Thank God for the girl who said that I didn't like myself and that I should go for counseling? Without her ever telling me that, I would never have changed. The counselor told me that motivation follows action.

Before *Depressed Anonymous,* I was paralyzed. I couldn't even interview for a job. I had no confidence. I could hardly get out of bed in the morning. I would just mope around and never really get moving. I would pick fights with my mother. I didn't know what to do with my anger or frustration. I didn't know where to place my misguided fears.

But then I found a place, the *Depressed Anonymous* group. We were a small group at first. In this group, we all had a story, and we had to let it out. I thought that no one could be in as bad a shape as I was in. I thought everyone was perfectly happy. We started the *Depressed Anonymous* group about a year ago. We took one Step at a time.

Being depressed is like being in a deep dark hole with no one to turn to. Your friends don't understand you. People around you don't understand your mood changes. I was so lonely that I didn't know what to do about myself. I just didn't give a damn. Now my self-esteem is up. I finally believe in myself. *Depressed Anonymous* has given me all that back. My attitude is positive. Right now, I feel as if I am in recovery. I still go to the group because without the group, I get argumentative, and with the group, I keep on an even keel.

Depressed Anonymous is a spiritual journey, which makes you go back into your past, find the rubbish there, and let it go. Without the *Depressed Anonymous* group or a group like it, I don't think I could function in a world as I know it. I thank God for the people who have the courage to come to the group. They will grow and learn. There is no easy way out. You don't change overnight. You have just got to keep working at it. I have been in the trenches with nowhere to go. I find this very common in humans. Change is very tough for us. We would rather bear so much pain before we are willing to change. This black hole is a terrible thing. I wish no one would ever feel it. It is painful and nasty.

This is my short story. I was down and I was out. I really couldn't care at one time if I lived or died. Now I do. It really didn't matter. I met a great woman and decided to get married. I couldn't have done it without *Depressed Anonymous.* It's a wonderful experience. I'm learning how to take care of myself. I met a lot of new friends at *Depressed Anonymous.* It takes time to change. You've got to be willing to take time to change. It might not work for everyone. But without *Depressed Anonymous,* I wouldn't be where I am today.

- Bill

Appendix A

Suggested Chairperson's Guide For Leading A *Depressed Anonymous* Meeting.

Leader: (Each group member is encouraged to take a turn in being a leader). "Good evening, my name is _____ (first name only), and I want to welcome you all to *Depressed Anonymous*, a Twelve Step program of recovery. We are a self-help group where people with similar needs can generate new positive energies from networks of friendship and support, and give each other the strength to live each new day with hope. We are a self-help group, and as such, we are not professionally led and we aim to be self-supporting."

Leader: "I want to welcome all new persons tonight. We all hope that you find the experience here a most helpful one. Also, no one is required to speak at our meetings unless they choose to do so. When your turn comes around, you may say "pass" and we all understand."

Leader explains how his/her life was before *Depressed Anonymous* and how it is now since he/she has been coming to meetings and working the Twelve Steps. Leader begins with the Serenity Prayer and all join with leader and pray in unison. "God, grant me the serenity to accept the things I cannot change, the courage to change the the things I can, and the wisdom to know the difference."

Leader reads the *Depressed Anonymous* Statements of Concern:

1 - *Depressed Anonymous* is not a replacement for an individual's relationship with his/her therapist.

2 - *Depressed Anonymous* believes that if you are taking some medication, you should continue to do so until you and your doctor agree that this medication is no longer necessary. You must exercise your right to know from your doctor about all potential side-effects of this medication and any literature from the manufacturer that would be helpful to you, the consumer. It's your health!

3 – Since many experiences of depression are due to a real or perceived loss; divorce, death of spouse, loss of a job, health, cherished possession, or loss of a love, it helps to believe that as an active member of *Depressed Anonymous,* you can live through this period of depression and become the serene person you want to be.

4 – Anonymity is not just a question of our name. It's an essential element in recovery. It is helpful for the depressed to feel that they can come forward without revealing their identity. Perhaps even more importantly, anonymity stresses the unity of *Depressed Anonymous,* which depends on the acceptance that we are all equal in the fellowship. Anonymity reminds us to place principle above personality.

WHOM YOU SEE HERE,
WHAT YOU HEAR HERE,
WHEN YOU LEAVE HERE,
LET IT STAY HERE.

Leader passes the Twelve Steps around the group and each person is invited to read a step. Then the Twelve Traditions are passed around the group. Each person reads a Tradition:

THE TWELVE STEPS OF *Depressed Anonymous:*

1.   We admitted that we were powerless over depression and that our lives had become un-manageable.

2.   Came to believe that a Power greater than ourselves could restore us to sanity.

3.   Made a decision to turn our will and our lives over to the care of God, as we understood God to be.

4. Made a searching and fearless moral inventory of ourselves.

5. Admitted to God, to ourselves, and to another human being the exact nature of our wrongs.

6. Were entirely ready to have God remove all these defects of character.

7. Humbly asked God to remove our shortcomings.

8. Made a list of all persons we had harmed, and became willing to make amends to them all.

9. Made direct amends to such people wherever possible, except when to do so would injure them or others.

10. Continued to take a personal inventory, and when we were wrong, promptly admitted it.

11. Sought through prayer and meditation to improve our conscious contact with God, as we understood God, praying only for knowledge of God's will for us and the power to carry it out.

12. Having had a spiritual awakening as the result of these Steps, we tried to carry this message to the depressed, and to practice these principles in all of our affairs.

THE TWELVE TRADITIONS OF *Depressed Anonymous:*

1. Our common welfare should come first. Personal progress depends upon *Depressed Anonymous* unity.

2. For our group purposes, there is but one Ultimate Authority – a loving God who may express Itself in our group conscience. Our leaders are but trusted servants. They do not govern.

3. The only requirement for *Depressed Anonymous* fellowship is a desire to stop saddening ourselves.

4. Each group should be autonomous except in matters affecting other *Depressed Anonymous* groups as a whole.

5. Each group has but one primary purpose – to carry its message to the depressed person who is still miserable.

6. A *Depressed Anonymous* group should never endorse, finance or lend the *Depressed Anonymous* name to any related facility or outside enterprise, lest problems of money, property and prestige divert us from our primary purpose.

7. Every *Depressed Anonymous* group ought to be fully self-supporting, declining outside contributions.

8. *Depressed Anonymous* should remain forever non-professional, but our service centers may employ special workers.

9. *Depressed Anonymous* as such ought to never be organized – but we may create service boards or committees directly responsible to those they serve.

10. *Depressed Anonymous* has no opinion on outside issues – hence the *Depressed Anonymous* name ought never to be drawn into public controversy.

11. Our public relations policy is based on attraction rather than promotion – we need always to maintain personal anonymity at the level of the press, radio, and films.

12. Anonymity is the spiritual foundation of our traditions, ever reminding us to place principles before personalities.

The Leader invites a volunteer to read how *Depressed Anonymous* works:

You are about to witness the miracle of the group. You are joining a group of people who are on a journey of hope and who mutually care for each other. You will hear how hope, light and energy have been re-gained by those who were hopeless and in a black hole and tired of living.

By our involvement in the group, we are feeling that there is hope – there is a chance for me too – I can get better. But we are not the people with the magic pills and the easy formulas for success. We believe that to get out of the prison of depression takes time and work.

We have all been wounded in different degrees by the experience of depression. We also know that there is a method to regain control over our lives that is practical and workable. It is successful for all those who want to change their lives. Some of us believed that there was no hope and that suicide was the only way out.

In this natural world, one of the first laws is that all growth is gradual – that belief is the bottom line for all of us who are depressed and who want to get better. The more we attend meetings, the more we will learn and see the various ways to escape from depression. We also learn how important it is not to give up on ourselves.

Leader: "I invite each member in turn to share his/her last week's experiences with depression, and each person's sharing should be no longer than a few minutes in length. (The **Leader** will make sure that in this round robin that each speaker limit their remarks and save their more extensive thoughts for the discussion period. **NOTE:** The **Leader** will also have the right to interrupt a speaker in this period who exceeds the short time period allotted. The **Leader** will caution all speakers that this is not a therapy group and there is no need to go beyond the past week unless special circumstances dictate. It's the **Leader's** choice at this time.)

Leader then opens the meeting to the whole group. (If the meeting is the first one of the month, then one of the Twelve Steps is discussed. This is what is called the Step Meeting). **Leader** chooses the topic for this meeting, either from one of the Twelve Steps, the Twelve Traditions or a topic appropriate for the meeting. **Leader**, after an hour or so of meeting (duration of meeting time is group decision) will give each member a chance to say what he/she hopes to do positively for themselves by the next meeting. Each person states his/her activity goal for the coming week. Each member of the group also comments briefly on one hopeful/positive statement that struck him/her in particular at this meeting.

Leader – Meeting basket is passed around to support needs and expenses of the group. (Tradition Seven of *Depressed Anonymous)*

Leader makes announcements and one person volunteers to be Leader for the next week's meeting. **Leader** has members rise and hold hands as they close with the meeting with The Lord's Prayer, or any other prayer, poem, or statement which the group feels affirms their beliefs.

THE TWELVE STEPS OF *Alcoholics Anonymous:*

1. We admitted that we were powerless over alcohol and that our lives had become un-manageable.

2. Came to believe that a Power greater than ourselves could restore us to sanity.

3. Made a decision to turn our will and our lives over to the care of God, as we understood God to be.

4. Made a searching and fearless moral inventory of ourselves.

5. Admitted to God, to ourselves, and to another human being the exact nature of our wrongs.

6. Were entirely ready to have God remove all these defects of character.

7. Humbly asked God to remove our shortcomings.

8. Made a list of all persons we had harmed, and became willing to make amends to them all.

9. Made direct amends to such people wherever possible, except when to do so would injure them or others.

10. Continued to take a personal inventory, and when we were wrong, promptly admitted it.

11. Sought through prayer and meditation to improve our conscious contact with God, as we understood God, praying only for knowledge of God's will for us and the power to carry it out.

12. Having had a spiritual awakening as the result of these Steps, we tried to carry this message to the depressed, and to practice these principles in all of our affairs.

(The Twelve Steps reprinted and adapted with permission of Alcoholics Anonymous World Services, Inc.)

THE TWELVE TRADITIONS OF *Alcoholics Anonymous:*

1. Our common welfare should come first. Personal progress depends upon *Alcoholics Anonymous* unity.

2. For our group purposes, there is but one Ultimate Authority – a loving God who may express Itself in our group conscience. Our leaders are but trusted servants. They do not govern.

3. The only requirement for *Alcoholics Anonymous* fellowship is a desire to stop drinking.

4. Each group should be autonomous except in matters affecting other *Alcoholics Anonymous* groups as a whole.

5. Each group has but one primary purpose – to carry its message to the alcoholic who still suffers.

6. An *Alcoholics Anonymous* group should never endorse, finance or lend the *Alcoholics Anonymous* name to any related facility or outside enterprise, lest problems of money, property and prestige divert us from our primary purpose.

7. Every *Alcoholics Anonymous* group ought to be fully self-supporting, declining outside contributions.

8. *Alcoholics Anonymous* should remain forever non-professional, but our service centers may employ special workers.

9. *Alcoholics Anonymous* as such ought to never be organized – but we may create service boards or committees directly responsible to those they serve.

10. *Alcoholics Anonymous* has no opinion on outside issues – hence the *Alcoholics Anonymous* name ought never to be drawn into public controversy.

11. Our public relations policy is based on attraction rather than promotion – we need always to maintain personal anonymity at the level of the press, radio, and films.

12. Anonymity is the spiritual foundation of our traditions, ever reminding us to place principles before personalities.

(The Twelve Traditions reprinted and adapted with permission of Alcoholics Anonymous World Services, Inc.

Appendix B

The Vital Spiritual Experience of *Depressed Anonymous.*

"This work (birth), when it is perfect, will be due solely to God's action while you have been passive. If you really forsake your own knowledge and will, then surely and gladly God will enter with his knowledge shining clearly. Where God achieves self-consciousness, your own knowledge is of no use, nor has it standing. Do not imagine that your own intelligence may rise to it, so that you may know God. Indeed, when God divinely enlightens you, no natural light is required to bring that about. This (natural light) must in fact be completely extinguished before God will shine in with his light, bringing back with God all that you have forsaken and a thousand times more, together with a new form to contain it all."

- Meister Eckart (c. 1260-1328)

If we have "worked" the Twelve Steps on a daily basis, I do believe we now realize the value of surrender and the power that releases in us. Just by making a decision in Step Three to "turn our will and our lives over to the care of God, as we understood God" is the beginning of reconnection with life and with ourselves. Now, we are conscious how our own isolation paradoxically isolated family, friends, and loved ones from us. The more our friends tried to help us, the more we went deeper into the darkness. Our darkness and their inability to comfort us in turn pushed them deeper into their own feelings of helplessness and isolation. Many times, the desire to help the depressed pushes the helper deeper into the isolation of the depressed – mirroring the reality of the depressed person.

Often, my clients are referred to other Twelve Step self-help groups of people dependent upon their particular compulsion/addictions. Most people have been hurt in the midst of their family of origin and so the Twelve Step group represents a potential new "surrogate" family where the hurting members can learn new behaviors, be accepted for who he/she is, and possibly for the first time in his or her life, be nurtured back to life and healing. Nothing could be more supportive than to provide a group of men and women with the means to encourage their commitment to growth.

The Twelve Steps are the essential beliefs and at the very core of *Depressed Anonymous*. The *Depressed Anonymous* recovery program was modeled on *Alcoholics Anonymous*, which was originally developed to help men and women deal with their addiction to alcohol one day at a time. The Twelve Steps have been found to be a potent means of recovery for those who desire to free themselves from their compulsions. The Twelve Steps are basically a program of letting go of our compulsions and handing over our will to the care of God, as we understand God. Essentially, our program is a Step by Step way to change not only our addiction, but our way of life. Change happens when we choose to change. The fellowship of the group and our desiring to make changes in our life is what provides our life-giving spiritual experience. Many people get organized religion and spirituality mixed up. *Depressed Anonymous* achieves strength from spirituality without set creed, dogma or doctrine. All the program asks of a person who comes to the meetings is only to have a sincere desire to stop the compulsion of saddening themselves.

We make no apologies for our faith in a God that can restore one not only to sanity, but to serenity and joy as well. "We never apologize for God. Instead, we let God demonstrate, through us, what God can do. We ask God to remove our fear and direct our attention to what God would have us be. At once, we commence to outgrow fear."

- Alcoholics Anonymous

Depressed Anonymous bases its healing and recovery on the premise that once depressed persons admit that they are out of control, even to the extent of attempting suicide, they can come to believe that a power greater than themselves can restore them to sanity, while at the same time, making a decision to turn their minds and wills over to the care of God, as they understand God.

The God, as we understand God, is what appeals to more and more persons as we admit our helplessness over our compulsive, depressive thoughts, actions, or behaviors. We feel we have lost all control over everything, including our thinking. The depressed person is aware that their unpleasant thinking is a cyclical and spiraling process where there is never a respite. This obsession driven by one's feeling of guilt, shame, and worthlessness is the fuel that continues our own isolation. This experience is not so much a psychopathology as it is a way for the human spirit to comfort itself. The depression then is more of a disease of isolation and being disconnected than it is a biological disorder.

The Twelve Step program helps people to become God-conscious. It is in working the program, while making no excuses for the spiritual nature of our recovery. We can begin to attribute our new-found sense of hope and peace to the Higher Power. For the active member of Depressed Anonymous, there begins to glimmer in the distance the bright light of hope.

By recognizing how it feels to be depressed, more people will have the help and guidance that will get them through their depression. Lives will be saved as well. Besides reading the Twelve Steps at each meeting, the group learns on a firsthand basis about the "miracle of the group." It is in the sharing and getting connected with the other members of the group where one's recovery begins.

It is in the group fellowship that the depressed person begins trusting their members where they have admitted that their lives are un-manageable, and that they have made a conscious decision to turn their lives over to God, or the Higher Power. This new belief gradually removes the fear that they will never get better. This old fear, if we take it back, can create and restore that habituated negative language that recreates an attitude in our mind that we can't make a difference in the way we feel and act. Remember, language creates our reality.

Appendix C

How to start a *Depressed Anonymous* Group.

If there is a *Depressed Anonymous* group operating near where you live, you could go to one of their meetings. But if yours will be with first in the area, you might find it helpful to attend one or two other self-help groups just to see how they operate. Most self-help groups, as well as *Depressed Anonymous,* have literature about their work which you would find helpful.

Once you have three or four people who, like you, are struggling with depression and who want to set up a *Depressed Anonymous* group which will follow the Twelve Step program, you can form a core group to work out how to contact other people as to where you will meet, and when and how you will all share the work and the responsibility of the group.

Sometimes, a professional person (doctor, psychologist, social worker, psychiatric nurse, or a minister of religion) is keen to get such a group started, or would be most sympathetic if you asked for help to get one going. You must make it clear from the start that this is a self-help group. If the professional person wants to attend the group, it should be as an equal member of it (and not as its leader), or as an observer. However, in establishing the group, the professional may be able to help in providing a place for it to meet and advising about organizing the group's finances.

Again, when you contact your local mental health centers to let them know that you are setting up a group, make it clear that this is a self-help group, and while you would like their support, you do not want them to take it over. To contact other likely members, draw up a notice which states the aims of the group, who the group is for, the time, day, place of meeting, and the name and phone number of the group member(s) who can give more information about the group and who will arrange to meet and welcome new members. When you are depressed, it is often very difficult to go into a room full of strangers, so having someone meet you beforehand can be a great help. Send copies of this notice to:

- Local Mental Health Agencies
- Local Physicians
- Social Services
- Pastoral Care Departments of Church/Hospitals
- Local Ministers of Religion
- Local Radio Stations
- Local Newspapers (including free ones)
- Local Library
- Local Post Offices and shops which carry notices
- Beauty Salons and Barber Shops
- Other Self-Help Groups
- Consumer Advocates Groups (Mental Health)

Many people believe they are the only ones going through this painful experience that we call depression. When they discover that there is a group of people who feel as they do, this in itself can provide hope. In time and with regular attendance at *Depressed Anonymous* meetings, they will no longer feel like victims, but will reach out to be healers.

If surrender of our wills to the "care of God" is of the essence of the spiritual life, for anyone who truly desires to free himself/herself from a chronic and compulsive behavior such as depression, then the Twelve Steps can be our stepping stones to the path of a hope-filled life.

Appendix D

How do I know if I am depressed or just having a case of the blues?

Being depressed means feeling disconnected, isolated, and separated. Truly, depression or melancholia is the disease of our modem society. Our desire to isolate ourselves from everyone and everything when we are depressing isolates us from ourselves as well.

To recognize how it feels to be depressed, more people will be able to liberate and unfetter themselves from their depression. Lives will be saved as well.

People describe their experience of depression as being in some kind of prison. One man said that he was in a pit where the walls were of soft clay. One woman said that she was in a brick maze where there was no exit and the walls were closing in on her. "I'm in an infinite desert" said one man, "there's just me and a lone scrawny tree." "I'm in a cage" said one woman, "the bars are thick and black and there's no door." Inside this prison, the person has intense feelings of self-hatred.

Frequently, depressed persons imagine that they are going crazy, are crazy, or are being afflicted with some bizarre mental illness.

One of the beautiful things about a *Depressed Anonymous* group is that everyone has the same symptoms, feels the same pain and is relieved that they are not the only ones in the world with this experience. They don't have to go it alone. They also don't hear people saying: "Snap out of it."

The following list provides a guide for those of you who are attempting to see whether you are depressed or not. If you feel that you have a good number of these situations going on in your life at the same time and for a number of weeks, your melancholia might be indicating that you need to get in touch with persons like yourself by the fellowship of *Depressed Anonymous:*

- Wanting to isolate and be alone.
- Changes in appetite.
- Shifts in sleeping patterns (too much/not enough sleep)
- Waking up early in the morning.
- Fatigability or lack of energy.
- Agitation or increased activity.
- Loss of interest in daily activities and/or decreased sex drive.
- Feeling of sadness, hopelessness, worthlessness, guilt or self-reproach and possible thoughts about killing myself.
- Weeping/not being able to cry.
- Lapses of memory.
- Hard time making decisions.
- Fear of losing one's mind.
- Reluctance to take risks.
- Difficulty in smiling or laughing!

Dr. Dorothy Rowe, in her award winning book: *Depression: The Way Out of Your Prison* describes how people build their prisons of depression by holding the following six beliefs as though they were real, absolute, and immutable truths:

1 – No matter how good and nice I appear to be, I am really bad, evil, valueless, and unacceptable to myself and to others.
2 – Other people are such that I must fear, hate and envy them.
3 – Life is terrible and death is worse.
4 – Only bad things happened to me in the past and only bad things will happen to me in the future.
5 – Anger is evil.
6 – I must never forgive anyone, least of all myself.

As already outlined in this book, Dr. Rowe delineates the six main ingredients of depression. These beliefs, tenaciously held, imprison the depressed until that day when they make a decision to choose to remove the bars.

Dr. Dorothy Rowe, a clinical psychologist from England, has written nine books which deal with how we humans, as creatures, create meaning for our lives. She possesses an almost universal recognition and respect from professional and lay alike about someone who has done her homework on the human experience that we call depression. She maintains that depression is not a disease or an illness, but it is a human experience that is painful and isolating in nature. She points out that the belief that depression is a physical illness has the good implication that we are not to blame for our depression but the bad implication is that we could get it again, like a bout with the flu or another cold. Psychiatrists who believe that depression is a physical illness don't talk about curing depression, but about managing it.

The bad implication for depression, using a psychological model, is that we caused it ourselves by the way we think (our six immutable truths), live out our lives, and reflect on the world. But the good implication of this psychological model is that if we caused the depression, we can likewise un-depress ourselves. This is the approach Dr. Dorothy Rowe takes. This is why she calls depression a moral problem. We have to take full responsibility for the way we think, feel and act.

Depressed Anonymous bases its healing and recovery on the premise that once depressed persons admit that they are out of control, even for some to the point of having attempted suicide, they then come to believe that a Power greater than themselves can restore them to sanity, while at the same time making a decision to turn their minds over to the care of God, as they understand God.

The important thing is not so much whether depression is or is not an illness or a mental disorder, but that people have to take responsibility for themselves and their feelings. So many people think that since they are patients of a doctor, they must just sit back and wait for the medicine to kick in. The doctor will be doing these people a great favor to ask them what has been going on in their families, their work, or with those whom they love. The depressed consumer of medical and mental health services might then get it that maybe they have a choice on whether they stay depressed or not. The consumer might also begin to work on themselves, knowing that everything they can do to take care of themselves will gradually eliminate the symptoms that we call depression.

So often, those depressed are living out of step with their own expectations or the expectations of others, sometimes stemming back to early childhood. It would be great if the many people on antidepressant medication would start talking out why they depressed themselves in the first place. The pain might disappear with the medication, but the experience is still part of their lives and memories. Unless one talks about the experience, then the depression symptoms will indeed re-appear.

Depression is a growing global mental health issue according to the World Health Organization. The numbers of depressed worldwide is growing as old traditions and values among groups are being lost, blurred or forgotten. Families become more fragmented with more single mothers attempting to raise children alone. The world is becoming a crowded place. An aging society in our industrialized nations brings with it those physical illnesses that come with a growing population. Late life depression is a special concern for those of us who are advocates for persons depressed. We all need to be in the forefront in advocating that more awareness be given worldwide to the need for mutual aid groups which possess the spiritual tool kits which can prevent further individual relapses back into depression. To stay depressed is to stay isolated and disconnected.

The main effect of *Depressed Anonymous* is that people can come together and find the support of fellow depressed people, and they in turn will find the emotional nurturing and acceptance. They can learn the social skills that can help them gradually center life again with hope and heightened spirit. Once people realize that they are not alone, they then take hope that maybe they too will feel better. The beauty of a self-help group is that a person feels acceptance from the group. No one is there telling you to "snap out of it" or that your depression is all in your mind.

Depressed Anonymous, once established in your community, will gradually gain new members as word gets out that a group exists in which people who are depressed can come and share their story with others.

I believe that the general public needs to see that they, even though not professional therapists, can still organize Twelve Step self-help groups for persons in their area. Most communities are in contact with mental health specialists who would be happy to help set up self-help or support groups for community members and to meet on a weekly basis.

IS DEPRESSION AN ADDICTION?

Webster's New World Dictionary defines addiction as "… to give (oneself) up to some strong habit. …" Anytime you or I have a compulsion to repeat a behavior, be that a mental rumination or a craving to seek out an activity, be it the physical ingesting of a mood altering drug or ingesting unpleasant and mood altering thoughts, then you have an addiction. We believe the term: "saddict" is appropriate for any of us who had the "habit" or "addiction" to beat ourselves up with a continued stream of unpleasant ruminations (thoughts and mental images) about ourselves, others, the future, and our world.

What we are learning here is that the Twelve Step program of recovery can be used to overcome any compulsive/addictive behavior for that person who sincerely wants to get emotionally, physically and spiritually healthy. The beauty of a self-help group is that a person finds acceptance from the group. No one is there telling you to "snap out of it" or that your depression is all in your mind. The one thing that you will hear at the group meetings is that if you keep coming back, you will get better.

It has been our experience that those who keep coming back to meetings week after week always get better. Now that's some promise! I've been in the program for twelve years and I have not had a relapse in that time. I am un-depressed today! I give thanks to my Higher Power and the fellowship of *Depressed Anonymous.*

Appendix *E*

How to get in touch with *Depressed Anonymous.*

A real revolution is taking place in the area of electronic communications. With the rapid rise of persons feeling disconnected and isolated, that is depressed, we can't think of a better time for all of us to come together and form communities of hope. You will notice that information about *Depressed Anonymous* can be obtained via a website, as well as via phone and fax!

Our groups are sanctuaries, sacred places, in a sense where one can become themselves as well as share their hearts with those who understand. It is here in the group environment where you and I can find friendship, hope and healing. If and when you feel that you would like to find out more about us, you may contact us at the various sites and locations listed below.

If you are writing to us and desiring for our information packet, then please send us a stamped, self-addressed envelope.

Mail Address:
Depressed Anonymous
PO Box 17414
Louisville, KY 40217

Website: www.depressedanon.com

Email: info@depressedanon.com

Voicemail: (502) 569-1989

Appendix F

Depression Resources Catalog.

THE DEPRESSED ANONYMOUS WORKBOOK:
Working the Twelve Steps one at a time. (This workbook was formerly entitled: *Depressed? Here is a way out!*) This workbook is an excellent stand alone treatment guide for those who desire to leave the prison of depression. For anyone who wants to learn the Twelve Step way of recovery, this book is for you! This work can also serve as an excellent group discussion manual for those who attend the healing Twelve Step group that we know as *Depressed Anonymous.*
125 Pages

DEPRESSED ANONYMOUS:
This work serves as the "Big Book" for those who are following the Twelve Steps of recovery. The work is 173 pages in length and contains 31 personal stories of those who have left their prison of depression, thanks to the program of *Depressed Anonymous.*
173 Pages

HIGHER THOUGHTS FOR DOWN DAYS:
365 Daily Thoughts and Medications. This daily guide will speak to you with words of hope and healing.
255 Pages

DEP-ANON FAMILY GROUP MANUAL:
A manual for family and friends of the depressed. A manual which helps family and friends take care of their own needs while helping the depressed significant other take care of theirs.
75 Pages

TEENCARE!:
This is a special tribute to those TEENS who discover how to be a person who sets goals and has desires to do something great with their lives. This is a 15 session workbook where TEENS are guided in the various ways that they can prize

themselves. Topics such as co-dependency, peer pressure, self-concept and self-esteem issues are discussed. "Teencare" is about loving oneself.
45 Pages

SENIORWISE:
A program for those older and growing. This program contains a manual for participants as well as for the Leader of a "*Seniorwise*" program. Basically, it is a full program manual for those seniors who may experience late life depression and feel isolated. The process of these ten week sessions is to help the senior reminisce about their lives and share with those like themselves. The program provides needed fellowship and pleasant activities. It gets the senior connected. Packed with material on late life depression.
150 Pages

SEEING IS BELEVING – 15 WAYS TO LEAVE THE PRISON OF DEPRESSION:
This work is to help the reader work through the various issues that afflict the depressed individual. "*Seeing is Believing*" and the "*15 ways*" are extra incentives that over the years have been found to help the depressed in the recovery process. They also serve as excellent discussion topics. They also seem to be a natural accompaniment to the *Depressed Anonymous Workbook.*
50 Pages

SHINING A LIGHT ON THE DARK HEIGHT OF THE SOUL:
This small work allows us to ask the questions: "Who am I?," "What do I want?," and "Who is my God?." The work also looks at the way shame and guilt has influenced us.
40 Pages

Order Form

Description	Price	Qty	Total
Depressed Anonymous Twelve Step Guide and testimonials.	$15.00		
The *Depressed Anonymous* Workbook Working the 12 Steps one at a time.	$12.00		
Higher Thoughts for Down Days 365 Daily Uplifting Thoughts and Meditations for those in recovery.	$18.00		
TeenCare How to prize oneself.	$10.00		
Seniorwise Group program for those older and growing. Includes Leader's Manual.	$18.00		
How to Find Hope! A short lesson in living.	$4.00		
Depressed Once-Not Twice! Special Introduction to *Depressed Anonymous* for Newcomers.	$7.00		
Shining A Light on the Dark Night of the Soul A short treatise on how to remove the guilt and shame voice.	$5.00		
The Promise of Depressed Anonymous For those who live the 12 Steps of recovery.	$5.00		
Dep-Anon Family Group Manual A 12 Step Program for those whose family members or friends are depressed.	$10.00		
Believing Is Seeing? 15 Ways to leave the prison of depression.	$7.00		
I'll Do It When I Feel Better This 150 page work contains Ten Chapters. There is an introduction by the author as well as a first chapter giving an overview of the book.	$14.00		
	Sub Total		
	Shipping& Handling $4.95 per order		
	TOTAL		

Make Check/Money Order/Western Union Payable to: Depressed Anonymous
Send to: PO Box 17414
Louisville, KY 40217

Include:
Name_____
Address_____
City, State, Zip_____
Phone_____